May you always
from deep roots
underground stre
                    and may you know.

Grain in Winter

To Margot & Iain

God's deep peace be with you,

Love,
    Beth

28·10·99

Donald Eadie

Grain in Winter

Reflections for Saturday People

EPWORTH PRESS

ISBN 0 7162 0524 6

First published 1999
by Epworth Press
20 Ivatt Way
Peterborough, PE3 7PG

Typeset by
Rowland Phototypesetting Limited,
Bury St Edmunds, Suffolk
Printed and bound in Great Britain by
Biddles Limited, Guildford and Kings Lynn

one way of saying thank you
to
my mother, father and my brother John

Contents

Contents

A note of thanks

I am grateful to those who have encouraged me both to believe in and work with my own writing when I have been tempted to offer an anthology of other people's crafted wisdom. I am indebted to Sue Whittle who typed what must have seemed to be an endless number of tapes, dictated when I lay flat on my back for such a long time. Marilyn Dimond has typed and corrected the various drafts of this book and encouraged me to stay with it. Grev. Ferry has helped me to find a way of lying and working with the new PC in the final stages of preparation. Valerie Edden, in particular, affirmed this enterprise from the outset and also provided detailed scrutiny of what has haltingly emerged. There have been others who have been companions through the whole process of shaping and reshaping material. The influence of Michael Wilson will soon become evident to the reader. Less obvious is the effect on this script by Tessa Lee. She has been a soul friend, encouraging, rigorous and gentle. Both Michael and Tessa have been companions during their own terminal illness with cancer. My wife Kerstin and daughters Nicola and Annika have borne with my frustrations and

believed that the struggle could be creative! We have
been through a lot together and no doubt there is more
to come!

Preface

Who is this book for and how might it be used?

It is for those of us who are learning to wait and move through times of change, welcome and unwelcome, expected and unexpected. Significant change comes in a variety of circumstances. For some the process is short whilst for others it is long-term. Both are important. Often the need for change emerges within one of life's transitional periods: the early years of motherhood and fatherhood, ill health, unemployment, redundancy, early retirement, separation, divorce, bereavement and the frailty that comes from ageing that sometimes includes failing eyesight, hearing and mobility.

Few of us come to terms with waiting ! We want endings and beginnings to fit cosily and flow easily together. Life is seldom like that! There is a waiting that is almost beyond our enduring. It can be a waiting within which certain illusions are necessarily shattered and romantic hopes shaken off. Only slowly do we grow into a new way of being who we are within the realities of circumstances that we often do not find it easy to bear. There are also times when we should stop waiting and move on.

Preface

This book is for those who want to reflect on the inner meaning of things within the human story and do not always find that 'church talk' illumines their reality. It is for any who need the courage and affirmation to become who they are where they are. These are the people for whom holiness or wholeness includes the journey towards becoming more truly human.

So these are those I choose to call *the Saturday people*. People in a wide variety of circumstances learning what it can mean to wait within a sustained, bewildering and messy period of transition! There is a long Saturday between Friday, the day of crucifixion, and the Sunday of resurrection. Some choose to call that day Holy Saturday. For *Saturday people* that day can last for years and not twenty-four hours and rarely is experienced as Holy in the way some in the organized church would have us understand.

What is written in this book is not strictly mine alone; much of what it contains arises from letters and conversations with a diverse mix of people whose friendship and companionship have enriched my life over the years. Some of us search for a way without map or compass, without easy solace or obvious hope. Others slowly learn to trust, within the bewildering contradictions of life, the resource that they choose to call God. They testify to the one at the heart of all things, the wellspring of life, the source of wisdom and humour, passion and compassion, the longing for truth, peace and justice. Some have arrived on the borders of institutional religion, perhaps retreating from it, perhaps hovering, wondering and approaching. These people can be described as being at a new centre, the context for exploration and discovery. My own upbringing was in a Christian home and a lively enquiring Methodist congregation. From earliest childhood I learned the story of Jesus and was encouraged to learn what it means to live the way he taught. His life, death and resurrection, I was told, were like a window illuminating the character of God. This I still believe. There are those who have greatly influenced my life who do not see things as I do nor use the same language to describe what is real for them. God is also sought outside the confines of the Christian church. God comes to us in diverse ways.

The last five years, for me, have included long periods of waiting between three spinal operations, a time when I have begun to learn where and in whom I can place trust, and slowly discern the markings of those people who are real rather than religious, resonating an authentic humanity. Whilst living through these times of waiting, I have drawn upon what I have written in notebooks through the years, stories, reflections, phrases, poems, prayers and bits of borrowed wisdom. This book is the result. Many of the stories and most of the reflections in this writing have emerged during formative periods in my life. In 1972 our family moved into Notting Hill in West London. It was a densely populated area, shared by people of a wide variety of national backgrounds and differing faith communities. For ten years I was a member of the Ecumenical Group Ministry based on the Methodist Church there. Since then there have been a number of significant journeys. During Easter time 1983 I visited the Caribbean with our younger daughter and stayed with the families and friends of people in Notting Hill. Four years later my wife and I spent three months in the depths of a very cold winter in her home country of Sweden. We visited community projects engaged with the large refugee and immigrant population in Stockholm, Uppsala, Gothenburg and Malmö. For nine years I was Chairman of the Birmingham District, an area covering five Anglican Dioceses. I travelled the roads meeting people in the villages of the Black Mountains, the Shire Towns of Worcestershire and Warwickshire, the urban multicultural and multi-faith communities in Coventry and Birmingham.

Among the pile on the table by my bed during prolonged periods of convalescence has been a white bucket, a gift from a discerning friend. It was given as a reminder that it is appropriate to tell things as they are and to resist the urge towards an inappropriate worthiness, heroism, and piety. This white bucket has become a symbol of my need to spit out frustration. The intensity of those feelings may have surprised some of my more reverend visitors! A monk, whom I have known for many years, asked, 'Donald, I hope you are learning to say "Bloody Hell"?' The white bucket now contains a flowering plant! A friend once prayed, 'Lord, grant that fruit that alone yields from frustration!' This book is the product of much scribbling into numerous notebooks and also much swearing into that white bucket!

What I have written may, I hope, provide some echoes of what is real for you. I want to encourage the discovery of God in our humanity rather than in our religiosity. I would like to feel that this book could be put into the hands not only of people who still talk of God and about the way of Jesus, but also people who experience themselves as on the edge, either retreating or arriving!

How could this book be read?

It could be placed among your clutter, notebooks and white buckets! I hope it will encourage you to jot down your phrases, bits of wisdom, poems, reflections and prayers that illumine the inner meaning of life, the wonder and perplexity. A lot of people write stories and poems but few share them.

The themes of 'Waiting', 'Trusting' and 'Marking' provide the framework of this book. Each section has the same pattern: stories, reflections, bits of borrowed wisdom and prayers. So you know where to look for what you seek!

I have included prayers. Some are from other people and others emerge from my own praying. There are as many ways of praying as there are people and each of us may pray in different ways at different stages of our life.

I have been influenced by those who encourage us to imagine that we see Jesus standing before us. He is look-ing at us. Saint Teresa of Avila adds, 'notice him looking at you, lovingly and humbly. Christ looks at you with love: looks at you with humility.' Slowly I am learning not only to speak openly and directly about the things that matter in my daily life, from heart to heart, but also to pay attention to the One who knocks on the doors of our life to make us listen.

Prayer is much more than withdrawing into a corner and screwing ourselves up to think godly thoughts for as long as we can manage! Prayer has to do with seeing deeply into things, paying attention to where our creativity lies: what we experience in life that brings us to life. Prayer is about engagement as well as disengagement, about wonder as well as failure. I trust that this whole book can be seen as an exploration in prayer and not simply the few sentences in italics at the close of each chapter.

It is not intended that this book be rushed or read from cover to cover; rather it is a resource to ponder, to have around and pick up, take what you want, a bit at a time, on your own or perhaps to share in a group. My hope is that this book will become part of a more humane way of reflecting on our life and its meaning.

Some of what is gathered here has been for me as *grain in winter*. I trust that in time you will also discover that which is as grain for you.

Donald Eadie
Advent 1998

WAITING

I

Waiting

There are few prepared to wait through the testing terrain beyond short term waiting. The future that emerges from such a place in human experience can be quite different from that for which we have planned or perhaps prayed.

Waiting can be the most intense and poignant of all human experiences – the experience, which above all others, strips us of affectations, and self deceptions and reveals to us the reality of our own needs, our values and ourselves.

W.H. Vanstone[1]

He looked down from what seemed like a great distance, grinning, 'So you are in the waiting game?' I had been lying flat for a long time and was too weak to hit him! I had waited in the waiting room with others who were also waiting. Some had been waiting for months, many months, for surgery. When I was eventually admitted to hospital, within a matter of hours I was informed of a car accident and the need for the victims to have emergency surgery. I was told that I must go home, enter another period of waiting and return later for the operation.

He talked about the role of the Guru in the Temple. The Guru is one who sits and waits, offers people time and attention. He stays put. He spoke of the occasion when he took his mother to meet the Guru following the death of his father. With others they waited in a queue at the Gudwara. He noticed a limbless figure, a person that he couldn't keep his eyes off but felt embarrassed to be looking at. And then when it was their time to enter the small room to see the Guru, he saw sitting on a mat the same limbless figure – carrying the marks similar to the one described in Isaiah 53. What the Guru said he cannot remember now. What he does know is that both he and his mother felt different after the visit. Of that there is no doubt.

He was an old man. He came from Jamaica. He was known by many. From the middle of the morning until late in the evening he stood at the gate looking and listening, watching and waiting, and that is where so often I met him; in the meeting were encounters I think I will always remember. His face was lined with the marks of wisdom. We spoke of so many things.

I wonder if we need to rediscover the craft of standing at the gate and waiting and listening.

Waiting

He was an old farmer with a sensitive ear to the soil of the earth and had lived all his life within the folds of the hills. 'We are learning to live within God's time', he said. 'You see, God's time and our time, they are different.'

Like previous occupants of that house, we have grown to love the magnolia tree that spreads and unfolds in the garden. Autumn's wet winds bring the heavy leaves to the ground disclosing buds bound close to the bare branches, buds waiting for the worst that winter can bring and beyond that the waiting for the warm awakening of the spring.

What have I learned through this experience? I would want to say something about patience, waiting, silence, hope, healing, wholeness but also frustration, anger, resentment, loneliness, despair, pain and projections. And within all this, beginning to discern what is real and also unreal.

Perhaps the hardest phase within the whole journey in the past months has been the living with waiting and with weakness and wondering when strength will return and in what form.

There is a waiting beyond waiting that tests the wanting! Don't talk to me about waiting games!

Waiting

In the waiting what is the wanting, what is the heart's deepest desire? How can the weeks, months and years that lie ahead somehow be used to enable this to come into being?

The new for which we wait cannot be known or imagined or it would not be new, it is beyond our imaginings.

The journey through waiting travels through the territories of loose ends and the jagged bits of life that should not too readily be tidied up.

Learn how to ensure that the immediate does not take priority over the important.

Open-ended waiting is hard for us because we tend to wait for something very concrete, for something that we wish to have. We are full of wishes and our waiting easily gets entangled in those wishes. For this reason, a lot of our waiting is not open-ended. Instead, our waiting is a way of controlling the future. We want the future to go in a very specific direction and if this does not happen, we are disappointed and can even slip into despair. That is why we have such a hard time waiting, we want to do the things that will make the desired events take place. It was only when I was willing to

Waiting

let go of wishes that something really new, something beyond my expectations, could happen to me.

Enter a waiting that is long enough to accomplish a turning, yield to the process, be shaped towards what is emerging, turn deeply within what is most important, within the waiting trust the process. Wait long enough to be reshaped, let the hard times be for good.

The waiting can produce a cracking that reveals jagged bits that are hard to handle, a swirling inner regression, a withdrawal, a disappointment, a sense of uselessness and a lack of purpose. Somewhere along the way I recognize that this is how it is and this is what has to be offered as a place of turning and growing.

God has something in mind that we have not yet seen.[2]

With us all things are possible! With God things take a bit longer.[3]

Take the waiting out of wanting.[4]

Vanstone says that in the passion and resurrection of Jesus we see God as a waiting God.

W.H. Vanstone[5]

Waiting

Man must see his dignity not only in being a point of activity in the world but also in being a point of receptivity: not only in his manifold capacity for action but also in the many facets of his passibility: not only in his potential for 'doing' but also in his exposure to 'being done to'.

W.H. Vanstone[6]

... the word 'passion' does not mean, exclusively or even primarily, 'pain': it means exposure, waiting, being no longer in control of one's own situation, being the object of what is done.

W.H. Vanstone[7]

Love has another mode of faithful courageous waiting for a consummation not yet realized. Love lives not only from the ecstasy of fulfilment, but from a loyalty not yet fulfilled. Love realizes itself, not only in the enjoyment of completion but in the suffering of the Not-yet.

Our culture is grasping for immediate possession. We need to learn that God waits and bears with his world.

Daniel Day Williams[8]

Waiting

The person who waits to hear from God may in the long run walk more swiftly.[9]

Sometimes God waits until we have exhausted our human resources before he answers our call.[10]

Esther de Waal in her book *Living with Contradiction* writes about the patience of God, waiting and working for the return of his children, the patience of God which is no less than the paschal mystery working in us through the *patientia*, the suffering of Christ.[11]

> Moments of great calm,
> Kneeling before an altar
> Of wood in a stone church
> In summer, waiting for the God
> To speak; the air a staircase
> For silence; the sun's light
> Ringing me, as though I acted
> A great role. And the audiences
> Still; all that close throng
> Of spirits waiting, as I,
> For the message.
> Prompt me, God;

Waiting

But not yet. When I speak,
Though it be you who speak
Through me, something is lost.
The meaning is in the waiting.

R.S. Thomas[12]

To wait open-endedly is an enormously radical attitude
toward life. So it is to trust that something will happen
to us that is far beyond our own imaginings. So, too, is
giving up control over our future and letting God define
our life, trusting that God moulds us according to God's
love and not according to our fear. The spiritual life is
a life in which we wait, actively present to the moment,
trusting that new things will happen to us, new things
that are far beyond our own imagination, fantasy or
prediction. That, indeed, is a very radical stance toward
life in a world preoccupied with control.

Henri J.M. Nouwen[13]

Jesus, teach us to wait open-endedly.
Help us to cease our attempts to control and fix the
future.
Deepen our trust that something creative could happen
beyond our planning, dreaming and praying.

Waiting

God, the wheels of this process move so slowly and the clouds scarcely move across the sky. And I want it to be different.

Jesus, help us so to search, that we discover what waits to be disclosed. Help us so to trust, that we become part of what you wait to bring into being.

Jesus, you invite us to be pilgrims still when images break; when we want to run.
Give us courage to wait beyond the waiting.

2

Silence

Break the silence only if you can improve on it.[1]

One day I spoke to a group about the significance of silence and talked for fifty minutes!

Some of us speak much of silence; we long for it but also fear the encounter.

There is a place where the mist hangs low over the forests like a listening ear.

It is a place to listen for the sound of the wing beats of the birds, for the jumping of fish in the lake, for the breeze rippling the water, for the drone of the bees about their business, for the woodpecker knocking the door of the tree, for the lily nodding its head on the water, for the ants treading their industrious path.

The moods of creation are mirrored in the water and reflect our own.

There is such a place not far from a village set on the banks of a broad river in central Sweden.

Perhaps it is also within.

She visited the strangely silent streets around Harrods shortly after the terrible explosion in London. She spoke to the police on duty about the new quiet that had fallen after the bomb. She talked about the people who now faced choices in central London. To stay in? To go out?

She talked about her awareness that violence and destruction are not simply weapons of dangerous invaders. They are a part of who we are as people, part of ourselves. They must be faced and owned as such.

Breda is a Roman Catholic nun who was preparing to live and work in communities of great poverty in Latin America. She phoned one evening and explained that, away from the rhythm of the religious community to which she belonged, she was struggling in many ways, including her praying. She wondered if a few of us would join her once a week for a period of shared silence. We met on Tuesday evenings in her little room at the top of the Family Service Unit in North Kensington. She lit a candle, read a few words of Jesus, then gently and firmly began a period of silence for about half an hour. At the close she rose to put the kettle on for a drink before we made our way into the night. On some summer evenings she opened the window of her attic room to let in the sounds of the streets, dogs, cars, pounding reggae music and children at play. Breda taught us not only a way of being quiet within the noise, but also awakened a deeper listening for the One who communicates through the encounters with people and situations in the area.

It is strange how the solitary silence of Nelson Mandela was heard both so near and so far.

The neglect of silence can produce a build up and create an imperative for silence. Body and mind can combine together to bring us to silence.

I don't know how to describe this territory. It has to do with the availability of the holy place, the human need for a place of brooding, resting, quiet, a withdrawing within engagement.

Through the years I have watched some of my best loved friends leave our church and become either Quakers or Roman Catholics, explore transcendental meditation or make the journey into Eastern spirituality. Perhaps it's temperament? Perhaps there is something to learn as well. Perhaps we need to integrate the human need for silence, for mystery, as integral to radical social commitment.

Where is the centre of our life, we who travel to so many people and places, where is the centre within which we listen, from which we draw? And what of the centre within which so much meets and clashes, so much that needs to be integrated and offered, the centre from which so much flows?

Silence

Within the process of listening to people I discern the territory that I choose to call 'the long pause' that it is so tempting to fill. To wait through the long pause for that which could emerge sometimes yields a rich harvest.

Through the years I have heard people hovering at the doorways of the church testifying to the warmth of the welcome and to a purposeful activity. But they want more. They look for a renewed sense of the mystery of things, for liturgies sculptured by shared silence, for a community prepared to befriend the awkwardness and pain of simply being quiet, feeling through to the still point of the turning world, they look for ways of meeting with God and people that affirm that the experience of ordinary people is an arena for God's revelation, they look to have the traumas and joys of daily life given much more liturgical and pastoral dignity, they look not for certainty but to find the assurance that we most deeply grow within our weakness and failure, they look for an affirmation that our common place is holy ground.[2]

There is a link between the inner life and the outer life. The quiet of the morning is the sacrament of the given moment. Silence is an inner disposition, a continuing flow. Silence expresses inner disposition, deepens inner disposition.

How do we really find God in all this – both in the standing still and in the journeying on? It depends on our disposition and on our openness and willingness to hear and to see and to be constantly aware of God in our life, listening in the fullest sense, listening with every fibre of our being, listening in all the ways by which God is trying to reach us.

This will be not only in words, through scripture, but also listening through people whose lives touch ours.

If we stand still without moving on we are in danger of becoming static, of failing to grow, possibly even of fossilizing.

If we journey on without remaining still in our innermost being we are in danger of becoming a wanderer, someone who is endlessly searching.

If we do not continually pay attention to the One who is closer to us than we are to ourselves' we could fail to discern what is being asked of us.

I have discovered the poison that can fester in silence, the mischief of talking about people and not to people.

Whoever perceives silence as a route to escape or to consolation is in for a shock. Listening within silence is not a self-indulgence! Silence can be one way of making the journey into a deeper awareness, both of ourselves and other people. Light and dark, innocence and evil, good and bad, creation and destruction, life and death belong to who we are. and can be befriended as such.

At times I meet people who have the capacity through their listening to enable a deep inner listening and connecting. Mercifully there is no need for interpreting or problem solving. This is a most unusual companionship.

A quiet time will include proper interruptions and invasion, that is how it is.

Be so still inside you that you can listen at every moment to what life is offering you.

We are so busy, preoccupied with all our own concerns, so self-centred, and obsessed with our own immediate world that we miss the good things that God has prepared for us and that lie there ready at hand, waiting for us to see them.

Love the silence of winter when the flowers say nothing.[3]

Waiting

Let me learn the quiet of the evergreens,
The resilience of the robin and the starling in
    winter,
The concentration of snowdrops, crocus or
    daffodil.
Take me out of myself, that cupboard that needs
    spring-cleaning,
And let me remember the size of the moon and
    search the sky for it.
Count the clusters of stars, enjoy the rain's
    animation,
The energy of nature, let me now and then learn to
    be peaceful
And add a quiet to creation.

Elizabeth Jennings[4]

At times we look for a person who knows something of the mysterious presence at the heart of silence. Beyond, beneath, within all our listening is the presence of the eternal listener, sustaining, enabling, listening in (and to) depths we shall never exhaust or fathom.[5]

The greatest revelation is stillness.

Lao Tsu[6]

Be silent toward God and He will mould you.[7]

Silence

The 'work' of Christ consisted in His obedience to, His unswerving trust in, the silence He called 'Father'.

Nicholas Lash[8]

When all things were in quiet silence, God's almighty word leapt down from heaven.[9]

Lead us into the silence that can both listen and hear, into the openness that can receive, into the rest that holds us in your way.
Lead us within the mystery of silence.
Help us to hear the great silence at the heart of God.
Help us to trust the eternal listener in silence, the mysterious presence at the heart of silence that sustains, enables, listens within and to the depths that we shall never exhaust or fathom.

Jesus, you cried out in the silence towards the absent and the powerless God. You trusted God, even in that place of destruction that leads to dereliction. Teach us to listen for the silence of the living God in your body. Teach us what it is to catch a glimpse of the heart of God in this place.

Jesus, why are we so afraid of silence?

3

A silence beyond anger

I discern a new silence, the silence beyond anger.[1]

I first saw her standing in solitude amongst hundreds of black people. She was strangely silent. She gazed into the gaping earthen holes that waited to receive the coffins of some of the thirteen youngsters killed in the Deptford fire.

One Sunday the British Movement marched from Hyde Park through Paddington to the densely populated multi-racial area of Notting Hill. They chanted their slogans of hate for the blacks to get out. Meanwhile in Portobello Road members of the Anti-Nazi League assembled, also preparing to march and confront the British Movement. It was a provocative and explosive situation. Petitions and deputations to the police to call off the marches produced no change. Near to where the two marches would pass closest to each other, a silent vigil was held. At first it was a small group of people from local churches praying in silence. Slowly members of the public came and joined the group in this unusual silence. Up above police helicopters whirled, obliterating the cries of the marchers. Within all the noise there was a strange silence and we listened.

Heroka is from Japan, from Hiroshima. She was silent, but for a moment she broke her silence when our children asked her, 'What is Hiroshima?'

In broken English, quietly, she told them of that beautiful day, 8.15 a.m. on 6 August 1945; of how three United States B29 planes approached her city. One flew over the central region, dropping a single bomb from 31,000 feet into the centre of the city. It fell rapidly for forty-three seconds. At about 1,800 feet above the ground, near the industrial hall, it exploded. A terrific detonation spreading heat rays and radioactivity. She told how fifteen minutes after it exploded the black rain began. It lasted for two hours, a drizzle of radioactive elements fell for another six hours. Heroka spoke of the 200,000 people who fell victim on that day, and of the effects which many still suffer. She spoke of the Memorial Cenotaph: 'Rest in peace, man will not repeat this sin.' Heroka resumed her silence. She has now returned to Hiroshima.

He was slumped against a doorway. He was from Barbados, Chairman of the Carnival Committee. 'Conscience forbids me to be silent,' he stuttered, as he often did! 'In fact, I have never been silent and never will be.' But he was silent on that night. He was slumped against a doorway alone, exhausted, tears running down his face, left in the rain. Carnival was over. A quarter of a million people had been on the streets. The green police vans were still parked in side streets, waiting. The noise of the bands and the drums, the whistles and the pulsating reggae had given way to the sound of police cars and ambulances, helicopters and riot shields, to yells and screams. This time the hands of the police were clean. They had been asked to keep a low profile, to let the black stewards handle their own young. And the police kept their word, till finally they had to move in. And we all knew they must.

He looked broken, drained, physically and emotionally alone. He was alone in the rain. His bold plans lying in pieces among the cans in the gutter, reduced to an unusual silence. But even the most cynical who watched him saw. They heard in his silence echoes from the heart of silence.

He was physically big. At times he roared like a bull. For a period in his life he was the director of a vast building and community development programme. He was a man of passion, of tears and of anger. But now he was reduced to silence. His health and his spirit broken. Off work for nearly two years, laid off by the doctor, disillusioned, scapegoated, alone, reduced to silence. But his broken health had opened up a way through, for workshops, playgroups, community meeting places. Once he hovered in the doorway of the church, listening for the sounds emerging out of the silence, but he turned away. He does not 'name the name', but his body and soul carry the recognized marks. Somewhere there are the echoes that can be heard out of that silence.

Listen for the wing beat of the Spirit and the creative word above the abyss of our mounting problems.

Source unidentified

Jesus, outside the walls, you are silent.
Brother carpenters banging, orders snapped out to sol-
diers for execution.
There is weeping, wailing, then shrieking.
And you are silent.

Jesus, once you walked the ways unfolding the news:
The living God is here! Among and within, all and
everything!
This one promise to the wanderers of the earth is true!
I AM is with you, for you, in all your ways.
In all your ways?
But why are you silent now?

Jesus, amidst all the noise around and within, help us
to hear the silence of God among the silenced ones.
Lead us into the mystery of your silence.
Jesus, you are silent, silent still.

Waiting

Lead us into the mystery of your silence.
Help us to hear the great silence at the heart of God.
Help us to hear within that great silence the echoes, the
songs, the alleluias that bounce from earth to heaven
and back, rising from the dust of the doorways, echoes
from the rising crosses on our streets.

Jesus, help us to listen.
Help us to hear within the silence.

4

The everyday place

We offer the common place as holy ground.

Out of the window early one morning I could see the snow lying across the gardens and under the magnolia. The sky was grey with clouds. There was scarcely a movement in the early morning. The next day at the same time the rain poured down and had already washed away all the snow. And I saw what I had not been able to see the day before: under the magnolia an unfolding carpet of crocuses. They had been there the day before but I had not seen them in their frozen environment.

For many years he was a social worker in Notting Hill. During a period when I was recovering from a serious car accident he visited me and predictably sat and listened. Just before he left he spoke very simply and directly to me. 'You know, Donald, this experience could either destroy or create you.'

Out of the dust that we sometimes despise, fear and hide from can come new life.

Tell me of that place where you give attention to the inner sense of necessity, the context where you can listen to the aching of your bones, the threshold where you tremble, the place of faithfulness and betrayal, stagnation and becoming, the place of trust and fear, the place of setting out and staying put, the place where echoes are heard, the place where rumours of promise touch, awaken, tease and set on fire.

The tree stretches its branches towards the sun and its roots into the dark and hidden places. Both are needed for growing.

If you think that the breaking of bread has anything to do with washing your hands so clean that you are somehow worthy, then you have got it badly wrong.

It is as if eucharist is happening within the world all the time. The bread and wine are simply signs of what is constantly provided as gift within the common place. The liturgy simply makes this visible. God is passionately committed and present for every person. The gifts surround us all and are for all. To say that this generosity is somehow dependent on historical, ecclesiastical rituals is a travesty.

Walk through life with your hands open, eyes open, listening, alive in all five senses to God breaking in again and again in your daily life.

He was quiet, that is until he turned and looked me in the eyes and asked, 'Do you really believe that God's Spirit is present within the ordinary stuff of your life story?' We must learn to listen to the ups and downs, the highs and lows, to what can be learned from events and circumstances, learn to talk to God easily and naturally within ordinary things.

The craft deployed by Jesus was to help people to discover in their own circumstances and events God's presence and goodness. This is evangelism.

Your body is God's dwelling place and home . . . and as Archbishop Desmond Tutu says, 'to treat any human being as less is blasphemous'.[1]

Our testimony is that however damaged, hurt, abused your body, you remain God's dwelling place and home.

The divine presence is known through encounter, not proposition.

Waiting

The hands of Jesus transform what we dare to call commonplace, disclosing divine presence and the unfolding purpose precisely within the context we often experience as threatening, unclean and alien.

The Spirit is not invited in.
The Spirit is already deeply present, yet hidden.
The Spirit broods within the place of inner darkness and the space between us.

The nature of the Spirit is to brood within dark places, to work within chaos, to move within the stuff of the human story, to speak through our own words, to meet us as soon as we turn to meet each other.

The Spirit essentially blows as the wind, blows where it will, hidden, brooding within the dark territories of human experience, shining essentially through the usual, the ordinary, the common, breathing life into the very soul of the human story. The ground we stand on, though dusty, is holy ground.

I heard someone quote Nietzsche as saying: 'For a tree to reach heaven its roots must reach to hell.'

The everyday place

Was the pilgrimage
I made to come to my own
self, to learn that in times
like these and for one like me
God will never be plain and
out there, but dark rather and
inexplicable, as though he were in here?

R.S.Thomas[2]

Be gentle when you touch bread.
Let it not lie uncared for, unwanted.
So often bread is taken for granted.
There is such beauty in bread,
Beauty of sun and soil,
Beauty of toil.
Wind and rain often caressed it,
Christ often blessed it.
So be gentle when you touch bread.

Anon.[3]

If the incarnation means anything at all it means this, that God is reaching us through the material things in the world of His creation. In the eucharist we are given bread and wine, the whole world is potentially a sacrament.

Waiting

I believe that only one person in a thousand knows the trick of really living in the present. Most of us spend fifty-nine minutes an hour living in the past, with regret for lost hours, or shame for things badly done, or in a future which we either long for or dread. Yet the past is gone beyond prayer and every minute we spend in the vain effort to anticipate the future is a moment lost. There is only one world, the world in which we are alive . . . this minute, here and now. The only way to live is by accepting each minute as unrepeatable miracle. Which is exactly what it is – a miracle and unrepeatable.[4]

Jacob deceived his father, cheated his brother, ran into hiding and then made this testimony: 'Truly the Lord is in this place, and I did not know it.'[5]

There is a new atheism in the church. Those who behave in the presence of God as if there is no God.

Emmanuel Jacob[6]

St Benedict tells us that our way to God lies in the daily and the ordinary. If we cannot find God here and now, in our home and in our work, in our daily routine, in the things that we handle in the kitchen and the office, then it is no good looking for him anywhere else.

Esther de Waal[7]

The everyday place

Jesus, you speak to us through our words, you meet with us as we turn to meet with each other.

Jesus, lead us into the mystery of God's presence and goodness, the one God who is over all, through all and in all.

Jesus, deepen our understanding of your nature, increase our awareness of your ways.

Jesus, the first trembling, quickening and awakening lie within the hidden darkness, the brokenness and the chaos. Out of these depths the first blurred images begin to form. The earliest echoes are heard. The first rising and falling, rising and falling, and rising again. From these places flow the tears both of anguish but also of joy.

Help us to go to our daily place remembering that the common place is holy ground.
May the generosity and the humour of God flow through our frailty.
May the hand of God hold us in our trembling.
May we live within God's peace.

5

Waiting among people

It is important not to be too clear, life is too complex for much clarity and I think God understands life is like this.

R.E.C. Browne[1]

Soon after we arrived in Birmingham I was visited by a small elderly nun and a huge Baptist layman from Balsall Heath. They spoke of their shared vocation, laid on them by God, to work within the red light area. 'We don't call them prostitutes but girls with special needs. Every night we carry on to the streets not judgment, there is enough of that; we take two things: hot soup in flasks (and the girls gather round, cold and sometimes wet) and the news that God loves them, however damaged, hurt, abused their bodies.' You are God's dwelling place and home. And during the week this unusual partnership follow the women into court, take care of their children and, when required, look for a safe place for them should they want to break the pattern.

(A Catholic and evangelical testimony to prevenient grace that would gladden Wesley's heart.)

Waiting among people

I looked around the ward at the young Muslim struggling and stammering, the old man who had had massive surgery on his spine, George in the next bed whose sister had unexpectedly died ... and I found myself wondering. I wondered about the nature and ways of God ... I cannot accept the notion of a partial God ... one who simply responds to the particular prayers of particular people. The God that I discover through Jesus in the New Testament is alongside for good those who sense that they have nobody alongside them ... so what does this say about our praying?

One of the many insights which I have had through prayer, which in a way is the only reasonable explanation I have for believing God, is that God is untidy! The corollary is that the devil is tidy! God writes with crooked lines. The progress of each individual life is a gradual alignment with the will of God, who, untidy as he is, has a wonderful pattern which will eventually become clear.

Michael Hollings[2]

> Ring the bells that still can ring
> Forget your perfect offering.
> There is a crack in everything,
> That is how the light gets in

Leonard Cohen[3]

Like the man in St John's Gospel challenged by the
authorities, in the last analysis we can only vouch for
what we have experienced: 'All I know is this: I was
blind and now I see.'[4]

There is, the Gospel says, a testimony made by the poor
at the gate, by Lazarus who is covered with sores, who
would be glad to satisfy his hunger with scraps from
the rich man's table.[5]

*Jesus, lay your hands on our blind eyes so that we begin
to see the blurred images like walking trees.*
*Lay your hands on our deaf ears so that we begin to hear
among the cries of your children the peals of laughter.*

*Grant that the mystery may so possess us that we do
not need to understand.*
*Grant, O Lord, that we see you in all things, and all
things in you.*

R.E.C. Browne[6]

6

Waiting for healing

Pain has to be listened to in order to inform. Mercifully my GP initially refused to anaesthetize the pain. He insisted that I listen within this process and not avoid it.

Diseases are a strangled message.[1]

Waiting in clinics, day wards, waiting rooms and lying in a public ward with my name fastened to my bed, have been experiences that I have found difficult but would not exchange. This is how it is for people. Beside me, men in their thirties had waited for a year or more for surgery and wondered if and when they would return to work.

'Behind most backs there is another agenda.' These words of comfort were beamed by some strong person towering over me, searching my soul with an irritating grin.

My mind has an agenda that my body has not been prepared to co-operate with.

Some of us ask our bodies to bear too much. I sense that some women listen to their bodies. It belongs to the nature of who they are.

But who teaches men, young, middle aged and old men, to listen to their bodies?

I was encouraged early not to attempt to be too worthy. Be real and be honest.

It has been necessary, therefore, to find symbolic dust-bins to spit my interior 'stuff' into. I have to confess that this has been an important part of the healing process.

There are surprisingly few people who can cope with our telling it as it is.

I need no reminding that within the physical realities there are complex reacting elements, corporate and personal, to do with communities and their structures, to do with the nature of personality. Organizational structures can both enable and oppress, time has to be managed, stress has to be handled, conflicts can be avoided or faced and worked through. That belongs to the human journey for all of us. But who addresses and helps us to disentangle and interpret this complex world?

It is possible to speak of social disease in Western society, to recognize the sickness of soul in nation and

church, to work with people in a wide variety of contexts who are ill, and to pray for their healing. I have
done this most of my public life. But perhaps much too
slowly and unwillingly I have discovered that I also am
part of the social malaise, the sickness of the soul in the
church . . . I am part and not distanced from it.

I puzzle over what it is deep down within us that at
times allows those territories that are both negative and
destructive not only to be recognized but somehow mysteriously transformed. The harshness is not removed, it
becomes the context for deep growing. Why it happens
for some and not for others remains a mystery. This is
true both for individuals and for communities.

I have discovered that I needed my work more than it
needed me.

I have still not come to terms with my own deep need
to control the timing of the healing process to fit my
own pre-conceived programme.
   I have been slow in being gentle with myself, in receiv-
ing what is offered, in being pliable to where I am being
led.

I don't know where the phrase 'Savour the flavour of
the present moment' came from but for many weeks

in a confined space it became immensely important. I wondered at the folded leaves of sprouts, I watched plants wave in the rising air above a radiator. I wondered about the warm milk on my Weetabix and melting brown sugar!

Solace came seldom from those contexts from which I had been trained to expect comfort, namely Bible and prayer. My methods of praying just did not work. I switched off religious broadcasts because they irritated me and often left me feeling that the human condition is just not addressed. I was being offered religious frippery. Solace came, however. It came primarily at unanticipated times and through unexpected contexts.

A friend dying of cancer wrote with this advice: 'Don't mourn what you can't do, discover and explore what you can.'[2]

The process has included struggling with self-image. At times I am conscious of a resigned invalidism, at times I use tactics to avoid questioning, at times there is a defined heroism.

I caught a glimpse of the flow deep within all life and I don't understand the mystery of its ways.

Waiting for healing

I needed my sense of shame and regret to be taken seriously and not dismissed. I have got it wrong and needed absolution. So, when the sacrament is offered in a shortened form without the confession and absolution, I feel deprived and separate from my sisters and brothers who somehow find healing within forgiveness.

I need to feel the interconnectedness of body and mind, community and personality, outer structures and inner worlds. I don't understand their interconnectedness, but I recognize the deep belonging.

To turn towards the future is not only a solitary journey; it is about inter-relatedness with other people and together finding common purpose.

I have discovered that healing has to do with the willingness to grow from within what is emerging and this involves trust. The nature of that trust has to do with living with the tentative, the unsure, the frail and the unknown, searching at times for a crossing into the future.

Perhaps the prayers for healing in time uncover deeper levels than at first expected. We want healing quick, fast and now in order to return to the normality that includes all the ingredients that brought sickness.

Waiting

And perhaps a waiting that at times seems too long is necessary to bring us to the awareness of a need for a deeper inner healing . . . wounds of separation, disclosure of hurt, pain, anger, insecurity within the corridors of memory. And there are unconscious scars. There is a growing awareness of the interplay of the inner and outer, womb and birth, dark and light, knowing and unknowing. There is a transcending, an integrating, a lifting up that includes an unfolding and embracing of the wounding.

The journey is towards wholeness, not just healing. And this wholeness brings together a number of paths – the awareness of trees and birds, discovery of music, the exploration of novels, the enjoyment of people, the delight in creation – the awareness yet again that the prime vocation is to be real, to be human not religious. It is about relish.

Sickness and tragedy are, unfortunately at times, the indispensable messengers that recall us to our life's purpose.[3]

The organs of the body weep the tears our eyes cannot weep.[4]

Jesus, grant that healing that you know to be most necessary.

Waiting for healing

Jesus, I still find that question you ask unnerving: 'Do you want to get well?'[5]

Accept me, O Lord, just as I am, in my frailty and inadequacy, contradictions, confusions and complexities, with all those discordant currents that pull me in so many directions.

Accept all of this and help me so to live with what I am that what I am may become my way to God.

Accept the tensions and help me to hold them together, so that I may learn to live fully, freely, wholly, not torn apart but finding that balance and harmony that will allow me to discover my point of inner equilibrium.

Source unidentified

Lord of my life
If it must be that I am laid aside
Let me be laid aside for you.

David Blanchflower[6]

7

Anger

Christians in particular have much to learn about anger. They are not angry enough.

Desmond Tutu[1]

What we need is a bit more arson.

We stood at a street corner at the close of a long day of carnival in Notting Hill. There was the sound of police cars, fire engines and ambulances. The fires were burning in the shops and on the streets. The old West Indian lady turned to me and said: 'The fire is lit, Reverend, and this time it will run.'

They had no children and had been married for over forty years. For very many of those years she had lived with some form of cancer. Not long before she died the doctor in the Hospice urged me to help her express her anger towards God. And it all came out. She died, I am told, at peace.

Anger

I found the prospect of enforced early retirement in my middle fifties due to the condition of my spine very hard to bear. Within and beyond the swirling emotions of grief, loss, sadness, disappointment and frustration there has been anger. It had felt as if an opportunity was opening up to live an alternative way of being in a world obsessed with activity.

One of the central biblical images is fire. It speaks not only of divine presence but also of 'the anger of the loving God'. Anger indicates depth of feeling, depth of reaction within the heart of God. Reaction to that which twists, distorts, poisons, oppresses, polarizes, human beings and communities. Rightly we fear anger but perhaps we are not angry enough. There is a proper anger, an intense passionate energy that needs to be appropriately addressed and focussed. Much pain has to be accepted and endured but not necessarily silently. The craft we must learn includes directing the outcry in a way that can be heard by the deaf and more than that, directing the cry towards the God who has promised to listen, hear and act among the people. There is a dangerous sickness among the people, an apathy which wrongly accepts much suffering in society and between people. The root of this suffering needs to be recognized and the causes removed.

It is possible to hear the story of Moses but not to feel the heat from the fire that was lit. It is possible to hear the story of liberation but fail to recognize the blood dripping from the hands of Moses, the white horror in his face after striking the Egyptian soldier in the brick-yard when Moses saw him abuse the slaves. It is possible to hear the crackle of the fire in the bush but fail to recognize that this is the fire that releases energy within people to leave the safe and familiar place, and to set out towards testing territories waiting to be explored. It is possible to hear Moses stammering, trembling and groaning, 'But Lord, I haven't got what it takes . . . can't you leave me be?', and only in time discover that when a shrinking person dares to set out into the unknown to explore, that person is the one who makes discoveries.

I have been too slow to recognize the links between the destructive and creative potential within anger, the links between weakness and frustration . . . and the sense of summons that exists within these thresholds.[2]

God gave Noah the rainbow sign, no more water, fire next time![3]

In the beginning there was not coldness and darkness, there was fire, blazing spirit, fire, personal, breathing soul into the newly formed fragile film of matter, radiant word, blazing power, melting and remoulding, real presence, indwelling all things, and kindling lives, the very heart of energy. Fire coming down into the heart of the world as it is, God's presence in the universe has now become a living flame.[4]

Anger

To be angry is very good. It burns out things and leaves nutrients in the soil. You should always be angry at injustice and cruelty. But bitterness is like a cancer, it eats up the host.

Maya Angelou[5]

Jesus, you are angry. You walk into the special place, for safe people, and you are angry. Some choose to call your anger 'warm indignation', but you are angry, you ignite, blaze, you are on fire! You place your body in the tracks, strangely silent. Sometimes you write in the dust over a prostrate woman, sometimes you stand eyeball to eyeball confronting everyone and everything that distorts and disfigures, spoils and thwarts, paralyses and polarizes, poisons people and systems, fouls up community and twists our humanity out of recognition.

Jesus, you are angry. You react directly and messily where woman and men are diminished, reduced to less than who we are, shovelled into the belief that we are nobody and nothing, compelled to fit in with other people's plans and policies, other people's pleasures, left to sit on what feels like time bombs waiting to erupt, left with festering wounds waiting to be opened for healing.

Waiting

Jesus, you are angry with the church, God's so-called chosen ones. 'You are like tombs covered with whitewash, you look well from the outside, but inside you are full of dead men's bones and all kinds of filth. Outside you look like honest men, but inside you are brimful of hypocrisy and crime.'

Jesus, you are angry, but in your anger you fold into your arms the cast out ones, the ones who cannot cope, the ones who threaten, the ones that other people want to get rid of.

Jesus, in your face we catch a glimpse of the anger of the loving God, we feel the heat of the holy fire. We hear the sounds both of judgment and mercy rumbling from the depths among the people. Help us to see that fire that spreads everywhere, that pervades all things. Draw us into that travail that transforms evil into good.

Jesus, help us to hear the laughter of God even within the wounds and tears of the people, in proper, patient waiting, but also within the proper eruption of anger.

O God our Father, we offer to you the fears and anxieties of our hearts — the fears that these occasions create in us about our own mortality; the anxieties that these occasions create in us about our failures in love and *care, and our inabilities to forgive and to receive forgiveness. We offer to you all those occasions in which anger and exasperation have affected our relationships; and we offer to you those things which have been done and cannot now be undone which have caused hurt and pain and misunderstandings.*[6]

8

Travail

Reflecting on the Gulf War: 'We are now in an Old Testament situation, polarizing good and evil, and this is leaving some people very uncomfortable. We know that we are caught up in both.'[1]

On a visit to the Caribbean a few years ago I asked, 'Who are your prophets? What are they saying and what is happening to them?' The response in each island was the same name, a man who spoke out clearly at the time of the invasion of Grenada by the United States. In the speaking out he was promptly called into the Government office in Bridgetown, Barbados, requiring that he be silent. Later some members of the churches required that he be not permitted to preach from their pulpits.

The same questions when asked in Britain produce a strange silence.[2]

Prophecy is about discernment, seeing clearly what is happening in society, perhaps too clearly for comfort, seeing beneath the surface of events, seeing through illusions and phoney claims, showing forth what we prefer to keep hidden. Prophecy is about expressing an anguish that must not be suppressed or be denied, both for and towards the deaf in ways that they can hear. Prophecy is about public signs, disturbing and offending, requiring attention, response and decision. Prophecy is about the celebration of the signs of the new creation within the travail of the old.

People are shouting, very loud, and those who ought to hear have their ears plugged and wonder at the silence.

The testimony within the almost unbelievable unfolding transition in Europe has been heard: 'God is at work.' But the same bewildering wind that has warmed the frozen European winter has also now chilled the unfolding spring, leaving many questions. Where are the signs of the Spirit in the creation of a new and common European home?

This must be a very confusing time for God, all these prayers for peace during the Gulf War from both Christians and Muslims.[3]

When I pray to God, I do not expect things to happen straight away, I pray with hope but God is not instant. We pray to God to show us the way to the goal.[4]

Waiting

May you live in exciting times.[5]

The priests no longer asked, 'Where is the Lord?'[6]

There is one who returns as Judge, identifying himself with the hungry, the thirsty and the homeless, the naked, the sick and the imprisoned.[7]

Apocalyptic is not about the end of the struggle, but about the unveiling of a new future.[8]

God's interaction with the world and his pressure upon events, then, is to be found at the point of the inwardness of things, our individual and corporate interiority. God is, as has been reiterated almost *ad nauseum*, the Beyond in the midst. God shapes what we call history through the inward response made to him by the leaders, the prophets and poets, and the holy and humble people, within the contingency of events.

John V. Taylor[9]

> To understand
> A little of how shaken love
> May be sustained

Travail

Consider
The giant stillness
of a willow

After a storm.
This morning it is more than peaceful
But last night that great form

Was tossed and hit
By what seemed to me
A kind of cosmic hate.
An infernal desire
To harass, to confuse,
Mangle and bewilder

Each leaf and limb
With every vicious
stratagem

So that now I cannot grasp
The death of a nightmare,
How it has passed away

Or changed to this
Stillness,
This clean place

That seemed unshakeable.
A branch beyond my reach says
It is well

Waiting

For me to feel
The transforming breath
Of evil

Because yesterday
The roots by which I live
Lodged in apathetic clay.

But for that fury
How should I be rid of the slow death?
How should I know

That what a storm can do
Is to terrify my roots
and make me new?

Brendan Kennelly[10]

The wind still blows through these forty years and more
The wind still blows through chill and lonely desert places,
The wind still blows to crack the hardened, poisoned
structures.
The wind still blows to melt the frozen wastes
The wind still blows and so it is
So it is for people, for nations and so it is for God.

*Jesus, within the breaking of the waters, both of the
womb and the side, enable us to hear not only the cries
of anguish but also the cries of joy and fulfilment.*

Travail

Holy Spirit, wind from heaven, blow us into ways not planned by us but belonging to your unfolding purposes. Holy Spirit from heaven, ignite the fire of your passion both gentle and angry. Holy Spirit from heaven, communicate across differences and preferences. Holy Spirit, speak to the soul of nations, communities and people.

Grant us eyes, O Lord, to see you in the needs of those who are broken by this world, those who are lonely, frightened in its turmoil, and teach us that, at the last, we cannot come to you without them. This we ask for the sake of your Son, our Saviour Jesus Christ.

Source unidentified

Holy Spirit, blow over the spoiled earth and renew creation,
Holy Spirit, blow among the torn peoples of the earth and form one family,
Holy Spirit, blow through your church and form the Christ that will be recognized only by its markings.[11]

9

Deaths in life

Perhaps this is the central mystery – the journey through death to life in so many circumstances.

Endings are real but they are also bewilderingly inter-related with beginnings.

The little letting-goes within life are but a foretaste, a rehearsal of the great letting-go.[1]

I was warned that leaving active work would in time lead to a sense of loss and grieving. In fact it has been harder to bear than anticipated. There has been a dying to an old life that embraced so much that I had wanted and loved.

And that has not been all! It has proved necessary to let go certain expectations and hopes that have sustained the turning into the future in order to find a new way. This has compounded the reluctance to let go and deepened wondering as to where it is all leading.

She is a doctor, well trained, trusted among the people. She is skilled in the art of modern medicine. She is attentive to the silence between and beyond words. 'But tell me', she said, 'of the nature of that life that lies beyond death.'

During the Conference at Swanwick with people from Jewish, Muslim, Hindu, Sikh, Buddhist and Christian backgrounds, one of the questions that began to emerge was this: 'What do you believe about the life beyond death?' The rabbi indicated that there was no clear mind within Judaism. Both the Hindu and the Sikh did make some testimony to the life beyond death. When Inderjit Bhogal (a Sikh who has become Christian) was asked that question he said something broadly as follows: 'I believe in the life beyond death but what we are given is a series of echoes within life. The child in the womb experiences that place as safe and secure. The child has no perception of anything else. The trauma of birth is profound and it is only by entering that trauma that they become aware of the growing life they now enter. Whilst in the womb there are only vague echoes of what is to come. The trauma of leaving the womb is a kind of dying to a form of existence, a dying that we call birth. It is a birth into a future about which we know so little but of which we begin to catch some echoes.'[2]

She was a young woman when she died, married with three children. She was a minister in charge of three small and in some senses unspectacular congregations. There was a simple family funeral for her, so it was decided to have a Memorial Service that would permit people to share their stories of what had become real for them through her.

Children were present. As people arrived the children gave each person a caterpillar cut out of cardboard. People wondered what was going to happen! Later they were invited, if they were so inclined, to leave their seats and quietly come to the table where normally bread and wine rest and place their caterpillar and leave it. In the leaving they were to be handed a butterfly. There is something really dead about the case of a caterpillar left after the butterfly has emerged and found its wings.

People who rarely speak in public, spoke. What wove through all they said was this: 'She lived her life among us and somehow we became alive to so much in the world, among us and within us.'

Amerindian man, when he is bereaved will go into the forest and choose a tree, he will then hit the tree several times with an axe, making a deep wound in the tree. This tree then becomes the man's special place. He identifies the wound in the tree with his own grief. The tree becomes a focus for his grief and whenever he feels the need he will return to the tree simply to be quiet, or to weep, or to remember his loved one who has died. Each time he visits he is confronted by the wound in himself. As time goes by he sees the wound in the tree begin to heal, the sap dries up, and the tree continues to grow, its leaves bud in the spring and die off in the autumn. Despite the wound which has marked the tree for ever, it continues to grow, life goes on. Slowly the Indian begins to heal, certainly the mark remains and he will never be the same again, but his life goes on, the seasons come and go and he continues to grow.[3]

The mystery we are invited to enter and explore and not simply talk about lies at the heart of all creation and within all people. There is a cycle of life through death, that is deeply in-built into all nature and human life. The process of death and renewal is the way life is.

The living of the last phase of the journey can be a coming to life within the process of dying; it can be a preparation for a home-coming.

Endings are endings and death is death and to collude with a denial of the fearsome reality of these territories can be a cruel deception. They are, I believe, the necessary crucible that has to be entered and endured.

I never thought that the springboard into eternity would be thus.[4]

Waiting

It is like being in the nets before a great cricket match. The batsman is relaxed, enjoying himself, but there is a sense of tension ... for something big is soon going to happen and 'Oh, I want to get at them.'[5]

You are on a journey and we don't know anything about the timetable ... we do know that there is a strong fellowship surrounding you here ... we do know that yonder there is a fellowship waiting to receive you.

Between the two fellowships there is a narrow way where it looks as if you are on your own but, even in a narrow way, you will have the presence and companionship of Jesus the Christ.[6]

He who pretends to look on death without fear lies. All people live afraid of dying, this is the great law of sentient beings, without which the entire human species would soon be destroyed.[7]

Certainly the dying individual shrinks from an unknown future, but also hopes for release into a fuller relationship with God.[8]

Biological death of body is therefore the ending of limitation, a door into a new form of being, a total surrender to the unknown with faith in God. 'Father, into your hands I commend my spirit.'[9]

Transformation from the old life into the new demands both a self-offering, and daily thereafter, a painful series of changes in perception, attitudes and values, which can well be described as a series of deaths through which renewal of life comes.[10]

There is always so much to be done and we are simply not equal to the doing of it. Our Heavenly Father never demands the impossible. That's certain. He, better than anyone, knows our limitations because He made us with them. If He wanted instantaneous results from our efforts He would give us the necessary grace, power and opportunity to achieve them. What is equally certain is that we of ourselves can do no good at all in the spiritual sphere except allow God to act through us. We could go through all the motions, preaching, counselling, visiting, but if the Spirit is not with us we shall be as successful as a radio announcer who speaks into the mike with the power off. I think our part is to put ourselves at the disposal of the Holy Spirit, and in our work to act as if everything depended on Him. We must do our best and leave the outcome to Him. It is a mistake to look for immediate results: we must go on working in faith, content to let God use us as he pleases. Remember: one person plants, another waters, but it is God who gives the increase.

I feel that He often hides the good from us that we do for Him to save us from becoming smug, complacent, proud. But I also believe that when we shall appear before Him to give an account of our stewardship we shall be very agreeably surprised at the amount of good he has achieved through us.

I also like to think of this life as the reverse side of a magnificent tapestry – just a crazy patchwork of colours and loose ends. But in front a design that astonishes and enthrals. At times we might well feel like loose ends that don't make sense, but the truth is we are strands running through God's design and forming part of the whole. When we go before God we shall see that plan and our part in it and we shall never cease marvelling at God's infinite goodness.[11]

Copying saints can be damaging!

'God meets us where we are, and not where we are not, or when we are only half there. God dwells where we let Him in. In another Hasidic tale the Rabbi Zusya said: "At the end, I shall be asked, not – 'why were you not Moses?' but 'Why were you not Zusya?'"[12]

Grant, O Lord and Maker of us all, that we may discern you through all the changing scenes of life.

When the signs of age begin to mark our bodies and dull our minds; when the ills which diminish us strike from without or are born within us; when the painful moment comes in which we suddenly awake to the fact that we are growing old and death stalks us; and above all at those moments when we feel we are losing hold of ourselves and are absolutely in the hands of great unknown forces that have formed us ... in all those dark moments, grant that we may know that you are parting the fibres of our being in order to penetrate to the very marrow of our substance, that you may bear us away that we may be one with you. And so our death becomes an act of communion.[13]

TRUSTING

10

Trusting

The wilderness in human experience is entered through an act of trust, not fear, a trust that knows there will be no safety nets, no sure happy endings, but there is a holding.

But to choose, with open eyes – even if it is in the dark! – willingly to bind oneself to that to-morrow which does not yet exist, but which is brought into being by the choice itself: that is perhaps the most difficult thing I have ever done in my life. Perhaps this is freedom.

André Brink[1]

He came from Dominica. He was a road sweeper. He was unable either to read or to write. Week after week he came to our home. Why? He wanted to learn to read, particularly to read the stories of Jesus. He had grown up as a Catholic with a liturgy in Latin and with the Bible remaining a closed book. I hope I will never forget the day when he stood up in church and read some of the sentences we had worked on from one of the Gospels. That was the first time I ever heard the reading of the Gospel greeted by applause!

Trusting

A young mother arrived at the door of the manse at the edge of a large housing estate. She explained that during her pregnancy she found herself speaking to one for whom she had no name or language. 'Tell me, am I going mad, am I speaking to myself, is there anyone there? If there is, can you tell me the nature of the one with whom I speak?'

An old man, wise in the ways of nature, told me: Swifts in the first week of August leave their young in the nest and migrate. The young are forced out of the nest in search for food. Born within them is an alarm clock telling them to leave these shores and a route map that leads them to Africa. It's called DNA, an information system in their chromosomes. Swallows are gathering in their thousands near the coast. They leave by early October. The martins are the same. Geese fly high. Swans fly low over the waves. Lapwings fly high to Ireland. Some over-fly and arrive in the USA! Birds navigate by the stars. Swifts sleep on the wing.

The process of letting go and trusting within the unknown belongs to the most crucial of all territories within human experience. Letting go is rarely easy. The fear is that having set out we could get lost, go under, get hurt, never return.

We may trust the unknown enough to enter it. We may trust the hidden hand of God to provide but not to protect from pain. We may trust God to renew vision. We may trust God to provide companions of his own choosing, not our selecting.

Sometimes in solitude and silence, in time, God's time, it is as if a spring arises from the dark depths, breaking through hard encrusted surfaces, flowing slowly, perhaps irrigating the parched territories of human experience bursting through and bringing with it jagged fragments from the depths in the releasing of what was blocked.

Sometimes it is as if there is a flow within life like a hidden river, a flow towards life, a well-spring to be trusted. Perhaps we have to learn again what it is to listen within life, to pay attention to what is being communicated. Perhaps we have to learn again what it is to receive within life what is offered as most necessary. Perhaps we have to learn again what it is to respond within life to the flow.

It was uttered with genuine intent. 'Lord, I offer you my life, soul and body.'

Then, as from the clouds racing above: 'If today is the day for strong language . . . then you listen to me: I am the one who does the offering. I have held, provided and always will; so stop the prissy offering stuff. And now go home.

Trust. And get on with what waits.'

Daubed on to walls in Notting Hill was a slogan: 'Save the centre.'

We look for a person who knows what it is to let God be God.

'I met people who trust God, not discuss God.'[2]

Intercession is an exercise in trusting God.[3]

The first step to healing is to accept the situation and trust oneself completely into God's hands – but it is difficult, isn't it?[4]

We may trust the God who permits us to make mistakes.

Trust the past to the mercy of God, the present to his love and the future to his providence.

Source unidentified

Trusting

Above all, trust in the slow work of God,
We are, quite naturally,
impatient in everything to reach the end
without delay.
We should like to skip
the intermediate stages.
We are impatient of being
on the way to something unknown,
something new,
And yet it is the law of all progress
that it is made by passing through
some stages of instability –
And that it may take a very long time.

And so I think it is with you.
Your ideas mature gradually –
let them grow,
let them shape themselves,
without undue haste.
Don't try to force them on,
as though you could be today
what time (that is to say, grace and
circumstances acting
on your own good will)
will make you tomorrow.

Only God could say what this new spirit
gradually forming within you will be.
Give our Lord the benefit of believing
that his hand is leading you,

Trusting

and accept the anxiety of
feeling yourself in suspense and incomplete.

Pierre Teilhard de Chardin[5]

At the heart of the Christian story is one who permits
himself:
On arrest, to have his hands tied;
On being sentenced, to be stripped and flogged,
One who let deceit and manipulation swirl around,
When broken and bleeding, God forsaken on the cross,
Trusts,
And invites others to trust,
and to enter within these uncomfortable paradoxes in
order that we discover within our own human weakness
the energy that flows from the heart of God.

(A friend commented 'Can it really be possible to trust
truth and mercy in this context?')

*Jesus, we bring our memories, our grieving and our
regrets for healing. We bring the mistakes we have made,
the hurt we have caused, the frustration we experience,
the uncertainties we simply must live with, the pain we
do not understand as places both of threat and promise.
Help us to trust in God's creating and redeeming presence, beneath, beyond, through and within all.
Help us to rest confident in God's forgiveness, mercy
and holding hand.*

Trusting

Jesus, your love leads us through all our ways, you renew confidence, you turn us towards the future, you call us out of our settled ways, you save us from despair, you lead us through life's struggles.

Jesus, you trust those who no longer trust themselves. You invite the ones who know what it is to weep bitterly, to be seen through, to be lost and in search of home, to be in need of forgiveness, the ones who know what it is to lie among shattered dreams, to be weak, to be hungry and thirsty, the ones who know what life is really about, what matters most, what good news is, what it is to be accepted as we are, to be trusted and to be claimed for ever.
Deepen our trust and hold us.

Today, good Lord, save us from being over-anxious about the world's pain and tragedies, about the future of the Church, about the immediate challenge of life, about the ultimate future of all things and all lives. Teach us to trust in Christ who carries the sins of the whole world, who is Head of the Church, the good Shepherd, the Resurrection and the Life, today and every day.

R.G. Jones[6]

II

Openness

The encounter with the Other through people of other faiths comes in many ways. For most it comes in the context of the everyday place – shops, health centres, schools, hospitals, bus queues and the work place.

Our first task in approaching another people, another culture, another religion, is to take off our shoes, for the place we are approaching is holy. Else we may find ourselves treading on men's dreams. More serious still, we may forget that God was here before our arrival.

Max Warren[1]

I was taken by an Indian woman to visit a Muslim family in Sparkhill. After initial courtesies the man of the house asked about the significance for Christians of the crucifixion of Jesus. There then followed one of the deepest and most rigorous discussions on the Christian doctrine of the cross that I have ever shared in.

A group of Moroccan Muslims came to the church wanting help. 'We need a place to teach our young the Koran, a place to meet socially, and we need money. Can the church help?' And, on this occasion, we were able to help with both.

The public rituals around our arrival in Birmingham included greetings not only from church leaders. We were also welcomed by Sikh, Hindu, Buddhist, Muslim and Jew. All of them came to the Selly Oak church carrying with them traditional salutations and prayers. The old Sikh, when it was his turn, walked down the long aisle, took off his shoes, bowed and reverenced the cross in a way rarely seen in a Methodist church. He showed respect for the sacred in an alien place that is rarely returned.

Two women from an Asian Women's Centre in Handsworth, one a Sikh and the other a Muslim, were amongst those who developed a special friendship and trust in one of our ministers. They asked if she could help them to know more about Jesus. She gave to each a copy of St Mark's Gospel to read.

One read it in one sitting and came back for more. This time she was given St Luke's Gospel. After reading it the Sikh woman returned. She wanted to discuss the different picture of Jesus in the two Gospels.

We wanted to launch a public appeal for money to help the Bosnian Muslims rebuild their Mosques, as a symbolic and practical way of demonstrating to Muslims in Bosnia our recognition of the particular injustices done to them; assuring Muslims in this country of our concern for their co-religionists; giving Christians and others in this country an opportunity to act on their concern for Bosnia.

We asked for too much! We were asked to withdraw the words 'rebuild their Mosques'.

I was informed that a few days later a woman, a liberal rabbi, phoned wanting to know if her Synagogue could send money to Bosnian Muslims to rebuild the Mosques through the Methodist fund. The money was sent but by another route.

A member of the Euro Women's Rights Committee joined a commission on a visit to Sarajevo. The religious leaders in Sarajevo have insisted on meeting together throughout the siege. The Imam has been quoted as saying, 'I could not see Sarajevo if I do not see the sun rise over my friend the Archbishop's house. He does not see Sarajevo if he does not hear the minaret.'

Those of us who are Christians and now live in a religiously plural society, what is our testimony to the God who does not practise particularity? What is our witness to the Christ who we believe illuminates the nature of the passion of the living God?

The notion in a plural society that we are 'all the same' is not only naive and romantic, but diminishing, dishonest and damaging. In reality we are deeply different in language and culture, personality and politics, lifestyle and role expectations. This produces not only rare human wealth but also real and frequent conflicts! Few of us like conflicts so we withdraw into a niceness for safety's sake! Wesley's testimony was to a 'catholic spirit, a heart enlarged towards all humanity, those he knows and those he does not, he embraces with a strong and cordial affection, neighbour and stranger, friend and enemy'. This is catholic or universal love. Martin Luther King affirmed: 'We live as brothers or perish as fools.'

I have been slow to learn that we are not all the same, despite having been exposed to people whose experience of life is so different and whose language and culture and educational experience is so varied. We are profoundly different yet we are held in the hands of God. And in a polarizing environment this is gospel.

The testimony is to more than tolerance, it is to an openness to search for truth, an openness to generosity and an openness to rigour within the roots of the common life. The craft is to seek the common good within our acknowledged differences.

Learning to live within the tension of outer public life, the possibilities, the expectations, and at the same time living the inner journey towards and becoming whatever faithful means. The being held within the bonds of inter-dependence . . . this belongs to the path.

Jesus, we ask for the help of God's Spirit.
Enable us to grow towards such an openness that we may be more ready to receive whatever God provides, both in times of pleasure and pain, in joy and trouble, in periods of rain and sunshine.

Jesus, make us communities of love that are strong enough and open enough to include others.

God, enable us to trust in your holding, unfolding and withholding hand.
Enable us to receive the gifts that come both in joy and grief.
Enable us to receive what you promise to be necessary for the living of each day.

God, you are one, make us one too.[2]

12

Holding

He sat on the floor of a home in Notting Hill, looking into his hands. It was the night before he was to return to South Africa and possibly to face arrest. Quietly he said, 'It is as if the wounded hands of Christ pick up the shattered pieces of our country and of them create a yet more glorious mosaic.'[1]

Jack was a potter in the Golborne, North Kensington. Each day people left the doorways and the lonely bed sits making their way to his workshop, carrying with them their many needs. Quietly Jack moved among them, frail, worn, grey, wheezing on one lung. He watched them as they worked with the clay and the clay worked with them. They found themselves, got in touch with an inner world that surprised them. On a Friday night some of the same people made their way through the dark, wet streets, this time carrying bottles and bis-cuits for a party. Laughter flowed among the wounds. Jack continued to watch over them. He would not call himself Christian, yet he had the face of Christ.

And there are people who are too busy for parties!

Trusting

The old man stood at the door of a church situated in a huge housing estate in Malmö, Sweden. Refugees and asylum seekers had made this neighbourhood their home. It was a winter day. He said, 'God has made us one family and through the Spirit is showing us ways of living together with our differences.'

This is the mystery we are invited both to enter and trust – namely the putting into the hands of Christ our broken images, sometimes those things that we would prefer to keep hidden.

The biblical testimony is that we are members one of another, made for mutual interdependence. Somehow within proper and improper conflicts, across deep political and cultural differences, a new way has to be found to debate the shape of the emerging future.

There is in the hands of Jesus a holding of contradictions, a holding of so much that we choose to separate, dark and light, judgment and mercy, gentleness and sternness, anger and love, threat and promise, endings and beginnings, grief and joy, contradictions held.

Growing towards maturity means learning to hold together the good and the bad feelings, the love and the hate, the frustration and self-assertion, the creation and destruction within one's self and within other people.[2]

The holding within the way of the cross looks crazy! There is a holding of people deeply different in personality and politics, people who don't even like each other, a holding after death of people who wanted to turn and run into hiding.

I have discovered that Shalom is not about the absence of tension but the creative holding within tension, the holding of diversity as a foretaste of what is possible . . . a sign of hope.

Conflict can be unpleasant but it is a necessary historic path towards oneness based on greater truth and holiness. It may be the way God uses to prevent a degeneration into a closed élite sect.

I have discovered that something is born from our attempts to face the truth together. But how to handle conflict so that it becomes a sign of hope, a sign of healing? The mystery we enter is of the hand that holds but does not hold on.

Let them go and they will return, hold on and you could lose them for ever.[3]

Christ did not come to make God's love and power the exclusive possession of the Church, but to reveal the nature of him who holds all beings in his embrace.

David Brown[4]

I hold and am held.[5]

Jesus, show us your way, lead us into your path, hold us within the new companionship, transform us into signs of your generosity. May the life that flows from the heart of God form and mark us.

Jesus, you offer your hands to lift and to draw us into the way.
Your hands are a sign of the holding and the unfolding hand of God.
Jesus, thank you.

'It is a terrible thing to fall into the hands of the living God.'
May the hand of God hold us in our trembling and lift us in our falling.
May the ravens from heaven carry food to us in our time of testing.
May our households learn the lessons of Nazareth, make the discoveries of Galilee, enter the mysteries of Calvary and Garden of Resurrection.

Holding

May the fire of God be kindled in us both to warm and
to blaze.

May generosity and humour flow through our life deeply
from the heart of God.

And above all may the Spirit seen to be at work in Jesus
be seen to be at work even among us.

13

Friendship

An elderly woman reflected, 'I have been attending church nearly all my life and still I am unsure what the word grace means. By grace do you mean the friendship of God?'

'I do,' I said.

She is an auxiliary nurse. Her face shows the signs of a severe hare lip. Her speech is impaired. She has had operations but is still ugly. Through the years she has shrunk into the shadows of loneliness and anxiety. That is until at work in the hospital she became friends with two other auxiliary nurses. Both are men, both devout Christians, both homosexual. Their gentleness helped her to discover her own inner beauty. Their Christian testimony led her to a local evangelical church where she was received with great warmth and was very happy. Her testimony, when shared in church, told of how she discovered inner beauty through the friendship of these two men. She said that she was won for the way of Jesus through them. What she said left some of the congregation confused. For her, their friendship has been an encounter with grace, for them it sounds like a puzzling offence. They told her that she

had a problem and needed counselling from the pastor.
Grace attracts and wins, but grace also offends.

'What would you say if I said Jesus is gay?' the old lady
was asked in a Herefordshire village. 'I would find it
very difficult,' she said, 'not because he was gay, but
because I need him to be heterosexual. I have been single
all my life but I wanted to marry. I have found in Jesus
one who responded to women as a man yet chose to be
single and that to me is important.'

I listened to them talk one night. They talked about
Hong Kong and its return to China in 1997, its relationship to Vietnam over seventeen years. Both came from
Taoist backgrounds, but in their youth attended Buddhist schools. Both had become Christian during the last
few years. What was it that brought about this deep
movement from within their cultures towards Christianity and caused such trauma among their families and
friends? It is clear that an old, quiet, and gracious
Chinese Methodist minister had been of great impor-
tance, as also had been the grace experienced among
the members of that congregation. The couple were
attracted and won by grace, by human kindness and not
by debate. They had encountered a love which in time
they traced back to the life and death of Jesus, a life
that they found in the place of hatred, a life that they
found in the place of destruction. This paradox has
claimed their lives. This is the mystery they entered and

wanted to explore. They were won by grace and not by argument.

For them bearing witness to Jesus Christ has included being involved with the Methodist Church in the protest movement, particularly the June 4th Movement in its attempts to work through the implications of Tienanmen Square in Peking. 'What does faithfulness to God require of us in our particular situation in Hong Kong? What does the calling to be Chinese mean for us as Christians?' they asked.

And I wondered how such perceptive, humane, well-rooted and nourished Christians are formed in such a short time.

Take good care of the paths between the houses, use them to meet each other. If they are not used they will be overgrown with thistles and become even harder to pass.[1]

The testimony of the Gospels is to the Jesus who is most at home with those who are not at home in religious institutions . . . He shares their lives, He speaks in language that they can understand. He helps them to discover both God's presence and goodness within their own circumstances.

Deep within the human unconscious there appears to be the notion that we must be acceptable to be accepted, lovable to be loved. This expectation of ourselves and of other people is not only unrealistic and naive but damages the human personality . . . It is a distortion of the welcome of Jesus.

When Synod was held in Handsworth we received as honoured guests the local leaders of the world religions, Muslim, Sikh, Hindu, Buddhist and B'hai. Earlier I had asked colleagues experienced in multi-faith affairs: 'What hymn would be appropriate to sing in such company?' I was not at ease with their suggestions. Eventually I chose Wesley's great hymn testifying to the nature and ways of God, 'What shall I do my God to love.' There is no need to apologize or to be embarrassed about the testimony to God's open generosity. God's love is immense and unconfined. God's love is for all, and God is present within all. We sang with immense warmth and joy. Afterwards one of our guests said, 'I was brought up in the Christian church but left in order to travel towards the Eastern religions. If I had heard the singing of such a testimony to God years ago perhaps I might have stayed in the church.'

I hope I will never forget the face of a friend whose life lay in ruins; her own self-image, her image of other people, her image of the church, her image of God, all lay broken into fragments. Her face was stained with tears. She came in order that she could share a discovery. Somewhere and somehow she had learnt, 'God has made our bodies his dwelling place and home.'

A terminally ill friend admitted that he found the language of a personal God, the human face of God, hard to comprehend, and yet near the end he testified that it was through the face of friendship, both of those who said they were Christian and equally those who said they were not, that he caught a glimpse of heaven.

It is incumbent upon every Christian congregation to ask: 'Who uses these buildings? Are they used to express the acceptance of Christ for the marginalized and alienated within society? Can this congregation risk misunderstanding and offence? Is it prepared to enter conflict? What gospel, what good news, does this congregation witness to? What is the testimony to the experience of the grace of Christ? Is there an open, warm and humane group where seekers can come, unsure of what words to use for the one for whom they have no name?'

There is among some a profound disappointment as they turn away from the doorways of the church. They acknowledge the warm welcome, 'Oh the church people were so friendly, but the worship was a vacuum.' Some still hover at the doorways of the church seeking meaning in a crazy world, seeking resources in a life that at times brutalizes, seeking a new and radical commitment within a society that many find profoundly offensive. Some seek one for whom they have no name or language yet believe that at the heart of life there is mystery. Some seek a vision for society and want roots to sustain that commitment. Some want liturgies capable of holding the reality of the jagged edges and the dark places of life as a context of the testimony to growth. Some seek a half-way house that can hold them in their uncertainty and lack of safety in their exploring.

God of the poor,
we long to meet you,
yet almost miss you;
we strive to help you
yet only discover our need.
Interrupt our comfort
with your nakedness,
touch our possessiveness
with your poverty,
and surprise our guilt
with the grace of your welcome
in Jesus Christ, Amen.

Janet Morley[2]

Jesus, you eat and drink with tax-gatherers, you invite not virtuous people but sinners.
You are gentle and also firm with the woman caught in adultery and with the scrounging crook.
You are stern and also compassionate with the long faced Pharisee.

Trusting

You enter the back rooms of our lives in order to lead us out into the light of day.
Thank you for trusting those who are frail, those who deny you and those who weep bitterly.

May the Spirit clearly to be seen at work in Jesus also be seen to be clearly at work among us.
May the Spirit renew this community within its frailty.
May the Spirit make of us a community where the lost are found, the blind see, the deaf hear, the paralysed move.
May the Spirit enable us to testify to grace, the seeking generosity of God, attracting but also offending all sorts and conditions of people.
May the Spirit kindle the fire of God among us to warm and blaze.

14

Turning

Through the years I have listened to people attempting to describe what happens when a person enters the unfamiliar places within human experience, territories that require not just looking at, discussing, but requiring a fundamental crossing, necessitating a trusting within the unknown.

I have learned for myself that the place of crossing is one of deep longing but also great apprehension. I have learned that the place of crossing can also be the context of disclosure. Timorous and tentative testimony is made within these territories. I regard this as one of the most fundamental of all human terrains.

I listen at times to young people who have travelled the world and recoil from the assumptions of the yuppie shareholding Britain, who want to live their lives differently, who are not comfortable within organized church life, who have no worked out political ideology or well-formed principles on lifestyle issues. They see much in the church that colludes with the general aspirations of society. I see in them a deep longing for turning into new ways.

I once knew a young man who was able, ambitious, perhaps even arrogant, self-contained and climbing fast, that is, until he was struck by a physical condition that limited him in a way that he had never known. Some say that was the turning point when he became human, learned things that can only be discovered in that place, discovered boundaries and received gifts.

Following the General Election in the spring of 1992 I recognized within both myself and other people what I chose to call 'a post-election silence'. We had glimpsed a threshold that could have brought us to a significant turning within the life of the nation. We had hoped that the process could precipitate a creative confusion at the centre of British politics requiring that moulds and patterns be broken, enabling something new to emerge.

What I hear people saying is: 'we have got it wrong, this way won't succeed, we must change our ways'. But how do we move beyond the whingeing and the whining, how do we move and turn within the social paralysis? I have learned that God does not wave wands over the vast complexities of the human predicament by simplifying and solving things. God does not work that way.

The word repentance is not one we are going to be able to use easily in public places. At the same time there is an awareness of *kairos*, a sense that the present time requires a profound response leading into a turning. What is required to release people into a movement towards the unknown? What language can we use to testify to rumours of life beyond death?

Repentance, I have learned, is more than regret, shame or sorrow. More than penitence. Repentance has to do with a deep turning and moving. Repentance has to do with a change of mind that leads to a change of ways. Repentance has to do with a letting go of old ways, a dying, a bereavement, in order that something new may be born, a learning of a new way into the future. These, I believe, are matters of soul within society as within individuals.

We live in a culture that silences people. We need stroppy people to rise up ... a deepening sense of outrage among ordinary people. We need people who will speak out about the truth of the situation. Where is the energy for change? Where is the alternative thinking? Who is doing the thinking about what kind of society we want and need to create? Where are the roots of vision and ideology fostered and nurtured?

I shared with others the overseeing of the church during a period when we attempted to address issues that both threatened and divided us. With others I learnt that the process itself can be a sign of hope. There can be no arrival without a journey that could frighten and transform us.

Trusting

... because you are not there
When I turn, but are in the turning, gloria.

R.S. Thomas[1]

Often in my life I have found that the one thing that
can save is the thing which appears most to threaten.
In peace and war I have found that frequently, naked
and unashamed, one has to go down into what one most
fears, and in that process, from somewhere beyond all
the conscious expectations, comes a saving flicker of
light and energy that even if it does not produce the
courage of a hero at any rate enables a trembling mortal
to take one step further.

Laurens van der Post[2]

Become what you celebrate.

Source unidentified

Until we act on our knowledge, we have not truly
understood.[3]

When we ask 'What shall I do?' – we are not ready to
hear the answer.

Source unidentified

The British want reconciliation, the Germans want an act of repentance.[4]

The middle and later years bring with them new thresholds. People seek new meaning and direction, longing, wanting to be human, still hoping that there can be a fulfilling of their years.

Sarah laughed in her old age and in the fulfilling of promise. Perhaps we should be setting up Sarah projects![5]

I wonder at times if there is a second conversion which draws us away from the centre of the church towards the borders.

The Jew Simon Peter was converted to Christianity through the Gentile Cornelius. Perhaps God's Spirit wants to break familiar patterns and structures and lead us into territories not of our own choosing and out of the shattered fragments to create a more glorious mosaic.[6]

The one we dare to call Gentile is often the one through whom God requires that we turn, change and enter into an unfamiliar territory that waits to be discovered. This is a threatening yet holy ground. The biblical testimony to Jesus is to one for whom conflict and confrontation seem to belong to the norm.

'A servant is not greater than his master. If they persecuted me, they will also persecute you' (John 15.20, REB).

To pray 'Come, Holy Spirit, come' could lead us through very unwelcome experiences, into territories where God breaks, creates and draws into a future that God shapes and we don't control. So, we must be careful how we pray!

> *We, paused on the threshold of the future*
> *Uncertain of its shape,*
> *Unclear of our role and perhaps tempted*
> *To cling to the seeming certainties of the past;*
> *Call on you to inspire our thinking,*
> *Inform our speaking,*
> *And amend our living,*
> *So that through us, in whatever way,*
> *The kingdoms of this world*
> *And this time may be blest*
> *With the character of heaven*
> *And addressed by the word of your Son*
> *In whose name we pray.*[7]

Lord God, whose Son was content to die to bring new life, have mercy on us your Church which will do anything you ask, anything at all except die and be reborn. Lord Christ, crucified in the world you loved between

two thieves and still suffering in our world, forgive us
that we so often choose safe ground from which to
commend you, save us from being engaged to be yours
but not found at your side.
Holy Spirit, reach deeper than our inertia and fears,
release us into the freedom of children of God.

Ian Fraser[8]

Jesus, make us explorers, give us sight of your footsteps
to follow, liberate us to live within your Spirit.
Jesus lead us beyond the familiar and the certain into
new territories.
Jesus hold us in the turning.
God of grace,
Grant us peace with Adventures,
Labour and a light heart,
A Sense of Vocation and a Sense of Humour,
A mind girded, but not tense,
Alert but not anxious,
Employed but not busy,
Strenuous but well rested.
In a word, Grace to you and peace from the God and
Father of our Lord Jesus Christ.

Russell Maltby[9]

15

The place of testing

There is a place in human experience, awesome in its testing, where security and protection are lost, roles removed, words come scarcely ... a place of awesome aloneness, so fearsome that companions leave ... and yet also a context of what some would call 'a cloud of witnesses'.

We are called to struggle, not necessarily to succeed.

At times I meet able, competent people who live their lives surrounded by the ambitious, in an achievement, success-oriented culture, and they refuse to play the game, refuse to push others out of the way as they climb ladders. Instead they choose to remain where they are, listening, caring, working at depths, making a testimony to humanity in what can at times be a brutal crucible.

And some will call this foolishness!

'Oliver Tambo was a devout Christian and always wanted to be a priest,' said Archbishop Trevor Huddleston. Who was Oliver Tambo? For many years he was the exiled President of the African National Congress. With others he worked for the transformation of South Africa, he struggled to keep the process humane and non-violent. He died, frail, in his eighties, after spending two days watching over the funeral rituals of Chris Hanni, the murdered Communist leader. He died within months of the first genuine democratic elections in South Africa.

He always wanted to be a priest . . .

And I wonder 'who are the priests and where in this world are the altars?'

I think my testimony would need to include the reality that I have learned most from those whose discipleship is lived within the acknowledgment of ambiguity and compromise. I recall a production manager, trapped between senior management and trade unions, handling the hard end of redundancies. I recall a bus conductress on the London buses, putting up with all sorts of abuse in her daily work and also living with considerable problems at home. I recall the director of a community development programme, a project aimed at reclaiming land for the local population. He worked with staff who faced public anger, complexities with local authorities, struggles with funding agencies. In a sense I knew him to be a lonely man, often misunderstood, but, in my judgment, a man of unusual prophetic depth.

Political activists in New York treasured the vocation of Thomas Merton the Cistercian monk. They said that he helped them to persevere when so many were dropping away ... He was rooted, he helped them to keep their balance and their own sense of reality.

When desperate times came, when they seemed to be accomplishing nothing, when they were calumniated, threatened and tempted to give up, it was Thomas Merton and others like him who salvaged them: 'We were not salvaged by the strategists or the sociologists but by men and women of highly spiritual dimensions.'[1]

I remember Desmond Tutu speaking quietly in Birmingham's cathedral out of the context of the crucible of South Africa. 'Light will overcome dark, good will overcome evil, love will overcome hatred, truth will overcome falsehood, hope will overcome despair.' And in this world this has substance and is good news.

If anybody else had said these words they could have been exposed as pious rhetoric.

The place of this mystic is not in the monastery but in the arena. He is no ecstatic dreamer sailing among the stars. He is no rhapsodist lost in rapture. He has the prophet's fiery soul which resents and rebukes wrong wherever he finds it ... 'There are theologians, preachers and religious leaders, not a few, who think that the essential thing about Christianity is to clothe Christ with forms and formulas. They look with disdain upon those who actually follow Christ and toil and moil motivated by brotherly love and the passion to serve. To them formulating definitions about the truth is a higher thing and of more value than to emancipate the underprivileged masses. They conceive pulpit religion to be much more refined than movements for the actual realization of brotherly love among men. Hence, religion becomes calloused and an empty cast-off shell. The religion which Jesus taught was diametrically the opposite of this. He set up no definitions about God, but taught the actual practical practice of love.'[2]

The new social machinery is giving birth to a monster that divides society into two tiers within education, health, social welfare, housing ... How do we enable women and men to live within their own territories with all the potential both for creation and destruction, environments that at times they find profoundly offensive because of their inherent ideological assumptions? How do we help people to live within these actualities and realities with proper anger and proper hope? How do we affirm and celebrate the priestly nature of those who choose to stay within these swirling processes?

Yet there is a chill wind blowing through our times and it is hard to articulate its nature. It goes something like this: 'Salvation in this society has to be earned. Don't do anything for anybody unless they are worthy.'

There are jagged and rough places where the powers of destruction and creation swirl, where people deliberately choose to stay and embrace circumstances from which they would prefer to withdraw, where people are reduced to silence and their bodies begin to carry the marks of the signs of the Christ, the passion of God. I have learnt that it is within these places that the quiet testimony begins to emerge as a spring bubbling up from eternity, with vitality, generosity and humour.

Has the time now come again for a more conscious developing of small groups that choose to listen to the scattered people, attend to scripture, discover again a worldly holiness, a breaking of the bread and pouring of the wine, a way of interceding that includes marking? Perhaps such little groups need to be available in unsafe places.

I have discovered too slowly and unwillingly that it is possible to face issues, speak the truth in love and work through to a new place. I have discovered that it is possible to disagree good-humouredly.

Being committed to God is not about being nice, it is about being real.

The place of testing

When in doubt, speak the truth.

Source unidentified

Christian devotion is more than looking back in admiration to Galilee, more than trying too hard to be good, more than attempting to be anxiously religious.

Christian devotion is about availability, making your body and soul, however frail and aching, available in order that God's Spirit may flow, form and mark with the signs of the passion of God for the good of the world.

And Mother Mary takes on a quite new significance, not the spotless, pure virgin some have liked to make her but a young woman in whose body, through whose travail, the interplay of Spirit and flesh form the One whom we recognize as the Christ.

And in such a place of trembling and trauma the Christ continues to be formed, passionate echoes of soul through the frail and fragile.

Jesus, help us to live the truth that we know with both courage and humour.

Jesus, show us, as we can bear, the marks of God's passion and lead us within these mysteries.

Trusting

Jesus, give us courage not to hide our faces when the tears flow.

Give us courage not to wash away the stains.

Release in us that breaking of the waters both of grief and joy that flow from the heart of God.

Give us courage to live openly with the stains of these tears.

MARKING

16

The body

If you trust truth, if you trust mercy, if you use good to overcome evil, if you seek to love those who hurt you, then you will also get hurt. This is what I mean by the marking by the hand of God.

So often I have heard these words, 'The Word became flesh.' Only slowly have I learned that this is the way God chooses to speak to us so that we can understand. This is the way God communicates with us, divine truth invading human personality, truth coming not through distant propositions but through encounter.[1]

Remembrance Day 1993. I arrived with my small case to be left in the ward at the Royal Orthopaedic Hospital. During the first hour I looked around assessing my new home. On television there was the broadcast from the Cenotaph. Wave after wave of soldiers, sailors and airmen, politicians and policemen, with church leaders in flowing vestments following after the Royal Family. The remembering of those who gave their bodies . . . 40,000 lost limbs in the First World War, 12,000 in the second. Above the noise I heard a sound and recognized the old man in the bed opposite was weeping deeply but quietly. The body carries so much within the process of transformation. Later in the day I caught a glimpse of yet another parade, this time in Berlin.

Three hundred thousand women, men, girls and boys in the march against racism. The human body bears so much for so long. Later in the evening there was news of the awful desecration to Bosnian Muslim women raped by Serb soldiers ... Muslim women carrying unwanted children conceived in trauma to be born into ethnic bewilderment. The human body carries so much. A generation of women carrying the babies of men of another religion and culture, children belonging to whom? With what identity? So what of ethnic cleansing?

What of the labour of creation?

What of the West African women arriving at Britain's airports carrying within their bodies hundreds of packets of drugs, packets that sometimes break and destroy the body?

What of Mary among the women weeping with their children?

Walking home one night after a rowdy public meeting under the A40 motorway in North Kensington, I listened to a militant community worker. He was a man bruised and scarred by the struggles of the area and also by his own particular nature. He was a man I grew both to admire and respect. Near the end of the journey he turned and unexpectedly confronted me. 'What I need you to be is a priest for me, not another ruddy

social worker, psychotherapist or community poli-
tician.'

I remember hearing Mother Teresa, old and frail, pleading to the vast crowds of Hindus and Muslims in India
that they listen to the call of God to love and to forgive
each other as the prime religious obedience beyond all
party passion . . . and on the same day the Israeli woman
barrister, a civil rights lawyer, pleading the public case
for the four hundred Palestinian displaced people, pleading with a passionate humanity for justice amidst a
swirling turmoil of religious and political currents.

The human body is the context of the disclosure of
the life of God.

'What is this marking of the body that you speak of?'
an Estonian pastor asked as we travelled home together
at the end of a long day. He was puzzled by the strange
language. The place of marking may be the threshold
at which we tremble. I begin to see people who trust
within the place of testing, trust truth, trust gentleness,
trust the unknown enough to enter it, trust the depths,
trust frailty and within these thresholds we begin to
enter the mysteries of God. This is the place of marking.
And I begin to hear the testimonies, the stories of other
people throughout the generations.

Remember wounded Jacob limping towards the out-stretched arms of the brother that he had so deeply wronged, Esau?

Jacob said to Esau: '. . . for truly to see your face is like seeing the face of God.'

Sometimes it is in looking into each other's face that we catch a glimpse of the face of God.[2]

The Presiding Bishop in Southern Africa talked about coming to God with the awkward questions: 'Why do the innocent suffer, the wicked prosper?' 'God, are you really there?' He made his testimony to Jesus not as some spotless, mighty warrior but as one who is wounded and brings the love of God into pain and despair. The servant is recognized through the wounding. 'Doctrine not rooted in devotion and practice is valueless.' He reminded us of the power of the figure in the shadows of Isaiah 53. 'God uses our suffering to speak to the world, God can bring healing from the wounds we now inflict, God will transform the world through the little ones.'

What is asked of you is not perfection but availability. What is asked of you is your 'yes' like Mary's, permitting life and love to flow from the heart of God, to flow even through you.

The body

Ministry is not about satisfaction, or fulfilment, but faithfulness, embodying the gospel that will both attract and offend.

Our testimony is to God, whose nature it is to bring life out of death, good out of evil, and it is into this crucible of human experience that we are invited both to enter and share.

We may trust the wind of the Spirit to open up a future that is of God's forming and not our plotting and planning.

We may trust God to make out of the broken pieces and the shattered images a yet more glorious mosaic.

We may trust the Spirit to mark both body and soul with the signs of God's continuing passion, the marks whereby the Christ is recognized.

You are the Christ through whom God seeks, transforms, laughs.

What the doctrine of the incarnation whispers to us is that God eternally wants a body like ours.

Source unidentified

Marking

The body is not seen as the enemy or as a prison of the Spirit, but celebrated as the Spirit's temple. My body is much more than a mortal instrument of pleasure and pain. It is a home where God wants to manifest the fullness of the divine glory . . .

Henri Nouwen[3]

Did the woman say
When she held him for the first time in the dark,
    dank of a stable
After the pain and the bleeding and the crying,
'This is my body, this is my blood?'

Did the woman say
When she held him for the last time in the dark
    rain on the hilltop
After the pain and bleeding and the dying,
'This is my body, this is my blood?'

Well that she said it to him then.

Frances Croake Frank[4]

Unless I see the mark of the nails on his hands, unless I put my finger into the place where the nails were, and my hand into his side, I will never believe it.[5]

The body

For years I have prayed with people in so many different contexts at the time of the breaking of the bread: 'In the Father's world you are now my body, held in the hands of God, for blessing, for breaking and sharing among the people, so that life may come into the world.'

It was said of the priest Alan Ecclestone that following the final prayers of the eucharist he genuflected, but not to the remaining elements on the altar. He turned and genuflected towards the people who became a sign of the rising and marked body of the Christ in the world.

A door was opened, linking the wretched of the earth, withering in their waiting for food and drink, to the one coming great feast, the feast that is for all to share . . .

A door was opened, linking the broken bread and the cup of wine to the shared human pilgrimage and the promise of provision of what is most deeply necessary for today . . .

There is a linking of the broken bread and the cup of wine to the actions of breaking and outpouring through people scattered to their everyday place. They become a sign of the rising yet marked body of the Christ in the world, a sign not only of suffering humanity but also of a deeply thankful people . . .

It is through the frail body that the generosity and humour of the living God mysteriously still flows.

Marking

Job could not conceive how God could be just and loving in a world marked by overwhelming personal suffering.

> You have granted me many blessings;
> Now let me also accept what is hard
> From your hand.

Dietrich Bonhoeffer[6]

Jesus, my body has brought to me such pleasure and such pain.
Help me to listen with care and to attend with respect.

Jesus asks: 'Will you enter these mysteries ... will you bear the marks which could carry the rumours of transformation, will you live within the way that many will regard as sheer folly, but a way that leads to the heart of God?'

> *A body is broken, blood is shed,*
> *A loaf is broken, a cup is shared.*
> *Jesus says to us now 'You are my body ...'*
> *To be broken,*
> *To be poured out,*
> *In the Father's world.*
> *So scatter to your everyday place,*

The body

the place that you dare to call common,
To live with humour and generosity
And to bear the marks.
You are free,
Free to scatter
And free to gather.
Go in peace.

17

The growing place

There are communities where only the strong, competent and able are encouraged both to lead and to perform. However, I have seen what can happen when the anxious, hesitant, inarticulate, unsure, discover from somewhere the courage to open up, at times stammering and looking around, yet offering something very special. In Notting Hill we used to call this 'buried treasure'.

When there is trust within the community, gifts can be not only discovered but shared.

A Swedish social worker said: 'In our projects we try and we protect the right to fail; here we grow through failure.'

A German social worker, living in Malmö in Sweden, spoke of his recent visit to England – Liverpool, Manchester Moss-Side, Brixton, Southall and the East End of London. I expected him to shake his head in disbelief and pity. On the contrary. He said that he was excited by what he called 'the signs of birth of something quite new . . . for when old structures and ways cease to work, alternative communities emerge. Social workers are then forced into new patterns of work.'

In Notting Hill we made mistakes, errors of judgment; we carried wounds in our relationships, but within them we also learned to celebrate God, who out of ruins creates a future that we have not planned, dreamed nor even prayed for.

I remember my expectations when I first visited the presbytery in Bayswater, the home of our new Roman Catholic priest. I had read his books, heard of his reputation and expected to discover a tidy and holy grotto! Then I entered his study! His desk was piled high with papers, emerging within the middle of the desk was an anglepoise lamp and around it swung a note, 'Lord, bless this mess!'

In a sense this is an image that expresses so much that I personally have found it hard to learn. Temperamentally I tidy up (though I don't think that is what my wife would say). I need loose ends to be tied up, I live with the illusion that if I work long and hard enough I will somehow get on top of things and life can be sorted out! I have found it so hard to live within the mysteries of mess – mess as the context of transformation.

Slowly I learned what it can mean to offer into the hands of Jesus not only what I am proud of, the good and the bright, the clean and the light, the competent and the strong, the noble and the worthy ... but also to offer the conflicts and the anger, the ambiguities and the compromises, the failures and the disappointments, not only as sources of regret and embarrassment but as deeply integral to who I am, the dark soil out of which God is able to bring the new life that we learn to call resurrection.

The world's salvation was accomplished within weakness and seeming failure.

Any view of ministry that is about omnicompetence and omnipresence is both a dangerous and a false one. True ministry has at its heart a testimony made within weakness and vulnerability.

God uses weakness. Perhaps weakness in the end will prove to be a profound gift.

I grow increasingly uneasy with the powerful who speak of 'the power of the powerless', the strong and well-protected who speak of 'the significance of weakness'.

There is a testimony that must be listened to. 'The saving work of Christ is fulfilled when He does nothing.'

The growing place

I have discovered the open hand can be nailed,
The sensitive can be humiliated,
The fragile can be crushed,
The weak can be mocked.
This is the soil out of which God chooses to bring new life for the world.
The open, tentative, fragile, messy, are all the characteristics of the birth for which God continually labours through his people.

We must offer the raw material, the unlived bits of life, the bits that we choose to leave on the shelf, perhaps deliberately, perhaps because they are too hot to handle. We must offer them because if they are ignored they will return again, sometimes knife in hand, demanding to be lived.

The invitation is to trust in a God who permits us to make mistakes.

It may be necessary to encounter many defeats in order to know who we are and what we can overcome, what makes us stumble and fall, miraculously go on.

Maya Angelou[1]

Marking

When we are born we are soft and weak.
In death we become stiff and hard.
The ten thousand creatures and all plants and trees
 while they are alive are supple and soft, but
 when they are dead they become brittle and dry.

Truly, what is stiff and hard is 'a companion of
 death'.
What is soft and weak is 'a companion of life'.

Therefore the weapon that is too hard will be
 broken, the tree that has the hardest wood will
 be cut down.
Truly the hard and mighty are cast out.
The soft and weak are set on high.

Lao Tsu[2]

Yes, of course it hurts when buds are breaking.
Why else would the springtime falter?
Why would all our ardent longing
bind itself in frozen, bitter pallor?
After all, the bud was covered all the winter.
What new thing is it that bursts and wears?
Yes, of course it hurts when buds are breaking,
hurts for that which grows
and that which bars.

Karin Boye[3]

The growing place

I wish I had remembered earlier what Jesus said to Simon Peter:
'Simon, I know you love me,
But I also know you will deny me, run away, hide in fear.
And this belongs within who you are, Simon.
In your place of breaking and weeping, in your place of failure,
This is where you will grow.
For the place of darkness is also the place of growing.'

Jesus, we offer you our memories, our grieving, our regrets, for healing.
We offer the mistakes we have made, the hurt we have caused, the frustration we experience, the uncertainties we must learn to live with, the pain we do not understand . . . as places both of threat and promise.

Jesus, lead us into the mystery both of mess and mass.

18

Unfolding

There is a phrase in one of our prayers of intercession that asks God not to remove weakness but 'within weakness to provide a strengthening'. I have prayed that prayer for years and only just begun to recognize its significance.

What I am learning is this: God provides but does not protect.

In a basement drop-in centre, open six days a week in the dockland area of Gothenberg, I listened to the project leader who worked with colleagues among people with drug, alcohol and psychological problems. They had worked as a team for seven years. I was told that between fifty and sixty people came into that centre every day. I found myself yet again asking, 'Where do these workers find the resources to stay in the place of testing? How do they remain creative, positive, believing in the future, in a place of doubt, disappointment, defeat and failure?'

Before she returned to Barbados, she looked back over the years in this country. She remembered the conversation around the font in the church in Notting Hill, a Bible Study on the book of Exodus and the testimony to the discovery of manna in the wilderness. She read her poem entitled 'Manna' to the congregation before she left.

She had worked for thirty-five years on the London Underground. On her last day at work she was called into the inspector's office at Edgware Road Station. Gently he looked back over the years with her. He made a cup of tea, then with others found a ritual to say thank you.

During the weeks that followed she carefully said her farewells to her neighbours and to people in the church family. When it was my turn she made a little speech. 'We'll meet one day . . .' and in the language she used there were echoes of a party, a great community meal in heaven to which we would all bring something to share with others. This image of the great banquet produces echoes in so many contexts . . . a homecoming, a sense of celebration.

During a family meal, after a long and tiring day, the front door bell rang. I was resentful about being disturbed. On opening the door I found an Afro-Caribbean man who told me that he had come in order to make a 'thank offering' to God. He handed over an envelope and later I discovered it contained £50 to be given to the church. 'God has provided and I have come to say thank you.'

Marking

There is a place for telling 'thank you' stories. I wonder, however, if we are reluctant to say 'thank you' when what is provided is not what we had hoped for?

The texts for the day told again the story of the shepherd, the sheep and the fold. Following the service an experienced social worker asked if she could talk further. 'Tell me more,' she said, 'of the nourishment found on the mountainside, the place where there are thieves, wolves and ravines. The sheep are led by the shepherd from the fold to the place where they could get lost and hurt. In those places they are watched over by the shepherd. In those places they find the promised nourishment.' For some reason I had not seen this before. For years as a city person I had assumed that the nourishment was to be found within the place of protection and safety.

'And what is this safety that Jesus speaks of?' she added.[1]

At times I meet people, people of vision and commitment, who have been nurtured in the church, who have set out to live their vocation within the testing places, but who no longer rest in our churches, and who choose to describe themselves as 'ex-Christians'. I wonder why they do not return to the so-called 'Oasis on Sunday'?

And I wonder about the wellsprings from which they most certainly draw in the testing places? What testimony waits to be heard there?

And again I asked myself: 'Where are the altars and who are the priests? Who are the stewards of the mysteries of transformation that inhabit these territories?'

In the longing for eucharist and for the eucharistic community there is an affirmation of the eucharist lying at the heart of all, an awareness of the sacred within all life ... and the need to discover and to live within these mysteries wherever we are and whoever we are ... a mystery of providing within unexpected places.

'You are to drink from the stream, and I have commanded the ravens to feed you there.'[2]

Bread and wine are signs of life poured out within a hungry and thirsty world. They are signs of God's passionate commitment within each and for all. They are a sign of God's promise to renew and sustain both people and communities in a search for a compassionate and interdependent companionship within the life of the world.

God provides minimum protection and maximum support.[3]

Marking

Beloved, you must find your own well, music's self at the end of thirst: it is not quenched by drinking at another's well.

Source unidentified

Jesus, your hands are a sign of the holding and the unfolding hand of God.

Jesus, you speak of God's generosity, the discovery of life within life. 'What you most deeply require for this day is already given, already around and within, already waiting to be discovered and shared. Your bread for today is given.'

Lord of life and love, we live in the promise that you know our story better than we do. Often we see nothing in our story but darkness and we long for your light. Hold to us in the darkness for the darkness is no darkness with you. Bring light to our story, the light of your healing providence, the light of the coming and creation of your kingdom, the light which dawns in doing your will.

(And a friend added 'until the light dawns grant us courage to remain in the darkness'.)

Unfolding

God, your love proved sufficient for Jesus when he
passed through death. Help us to go on trusting you
through every triumph and disaster until we rise in Him
beyond the reach of pain and sorrow. Draw us into the
mystery of your eternal glory.

19

Withholding

The testimony to God's providence is wonderful in its unfolding and perplexing in its withholding.

The God who is with us is also the God who forsakes us.
The God who permits the journey to the cross does not rescue us at the last moment.
The testimony to God's providing includes, I believe, what looks like the withholding hand of God. William Cowper has a phrase in one of his hymns testifying to 'a frowning providence'.[1]

The answer's no.

Heralding dawn
A songthrush is shot by a youngster for fun.
O maker of both
Could you not wobble the aim of a gun
For a song?
Two cars
Speed towards one another
Head on:

Withholding

The driver of one is asleep.
O patron saint of drivers
Could you not nudge him awake
Just in time?
A tiny child
Chases a bouncing ball
Into the road.
Drinking driver brakes too late.
O guardian angel of battered body
Could you not trip a toddler on the kerb?

Michael Wilson[2]

On returning from Uruguay a couple described their visit. 'We saw people living from food left over in rubbish heaps. We saw people daily searching through dustbins for food. We saw people with no prospect of work, perhaps for the rest of their lives.'

And I wondered: What does it mean to say 'God will provide' when some have so much and others have nothing? How is it that it is the poor and desperate, not the prosperous, who so often testify to the God who provides?

I have discovered a wealth among the poor and a poverty among the rich. I have discovered the Beatitudes from those that I intended to help. Life can be both cruel and unfair. At times God's providing seems bewilderingly selective and inconsistent.[3]

As a friend left my room he turned and said, 'Next time I come to talk with you I need and want to talk about my experience of "bridled providence".' I have never heard that phrase before or since. And he has never returned for that conversation.

The crossing at times has been rough but necessary. The storm has not always included calm at its heart!

Many do not want to believe the social realities that continue to exist in this country, both in inner and outer urban housing estates. Increasingly I wonder how loud the Magnificat should be sung and by whom?[4]

There has been within a constellation of events, an asking – followed by silence, a searching apparently in vain, a knocking at doors that would not yield, followed by a waiting beyond waiting within God's time. And there has been a prayer, familiar to many: 'Lord, I wish the way you want us to go would be clear, and when it is not, give us wisdom and courage to take one step at a time.'

Times of transition in nations, communities and personal stories are accompanied by apprehension and excitement – both. For me there has been a solitude within transition within which there is also a dawning awareness of a waiting cloud of witnesses, a being drawn into a new and given companionship. To have faith within transition is to trust . . . to trust within the bewildering world of paradox, of unknowing and knowing, uncertainty and of sureness. It is a time of ultimate trust in the resource we call God.

Trust includes paying attention to a sense of inner necessity, that which searches for nourishment and that which gives life. Trust includes paying attention to the call to bring into being that which is Christ within us.

God can be very destructive in the process of achieving His will.[5]

Ask, and you will receive; seek, and you will find; knock and the door will be opened to you (Luke 11.9).
  Jesus, this is one of the scary sayings. We are not sure if we want to receive, or to find . . . And not sure if we want the door to open. Jesus, stay close at the time of trembling.

For everyone who asks receives, those who seek find, and to those who knock, the door will be opened (Luke 11.10).
  Jesus, we don't understand this.
  Why does it seem to work for some and not others?

Marking

O God, the same yesterday, today and forever, though we sense your absence in a bleak despairing time, focus our minds and hearts on memories of grace surprising us, that faith may be kept alive and hope re-kindled.

Jim Cotter[6]

20

Life

Help us to wait longer than seems possible, in the place of shattered dreams until from somewhere there is a rising to new life.

'*We look for the resurrection of the dead.*'[1]
Do we?

They came scruffy, laughing and carrying little into what local people later called Frestonia! (an almost forgotten corner of London W12). It was a network of small roads, derelict houses, unused shops, surrounded and guarded by corrugated iron. 'Is there life before death?' someone had daubed. They came to occupy it. To set up squats, humane communities, alternative shops, play spaces for children and work projects for the un-employed. They dared to declare UDI! A rose in the desert! An angry yet humane sign of resurrection within dereliction.

He is black, Catholic and was with the Royal Shake-speare Company, that is until he had a terrible car accident. He was stopped in his tracks, shaken to his core, and for the first time in his life began really to search for both meaning and direction. His anger and bewilderment led him to an unwanted and derelict church hall in the back streets of North Kensington. He turned the tables upside down and with others transformed that drab hall into a black people's workshop. There were a hundred and twenty youngsters, some unemployed, some squatting, some running from the law, each of them taking off. It was like watching a beautiful black bird, powerful, creative, rising into the sky . . . music, drama, dance, reading, writing, black history, jobs, – a sign of transformation within a wasteland.

The testimony is that out of the darkest of soil God brings the life we call 'resurrection', out of the ruins of the best made plans, out of bruised and disappointed people, God brings the new creation . . . within a place of fear and trembling God still opens up in the deep places a future that we could not plan.

For some these rumours are sheer foolishness; for others they are the central mystery into which Jesus invites us both to enter and trust.

I have lived for too long with the notion that holiness requires cautious correctness, planned godliness, a longing for purity and the acceptance of certain well-formulated beliefs. Only slowly and painfully have I learned that these expectations of myself and of other people are not only naive and unrealistic but damaging to human personality. We did not learn these things from the Jesus of the Gospels. The clear testimony of scripture is this: 'Christ died for us while we were yet sinners.'

Only slowly have I learned that holiness is about the journey towards humanity, towards an inter-relatedness, about learning to live with ambiguities, complexities, learning to integrate light and dark, strength and weakness.

Only slowly have I learned that the dark and fearful places in human experience that I so often turn my back on, can become the dark soil out of which new life comes.

We are right not to trust too easily other people's smooth words about new life.

> Do not make the mistake
> of imagining that you
> may go singing
> on the Via Dolorosa
> neither may you
> bear right or left
> the way is confined
> with little room
> for manoeuvre
> You will know exhaustion
> kneeling often

trodden and rough
rough and scarred by many feet
this way is our way
and may not be shunned
turned from
or avoided
best to go quietly
with a dogged courage
knowing that
one thing is certain:
There is an end

And when you arrive
you will find
that the hill is crowned
with a living tree
stretching out
great branches
to give you shelter
and manna there
and spring water

Margaret Torrie[2]

One of the most poignant stories in the Gospels is the picture of the two men walking away from Jerusalem after the death and burial of Jesus. 'Oh, we had hoped . . .', they sighed to a stranger.

To speak of the renewal of vision without acknowledging the reality of that disappointment and disillusionment which leads to social disengagement would be to hide from reality. This is a matter of soul both for people and community. Christian hope requires that we painfully let go both false hopes and naive notions of progress.

Biblical testimony is that it is the very nature of God to bring life within the ruins of shattered dreams and failures.[3]

Behind the monastery, down by the road,
there is a cemetery of worn out things
there lie smashed china, rusty metal,
cracked pipes and twisted bits of wire,
empty cigarette packets, sawdust,
corrugated iron, old plastic, tyres beyond repair:
all waiting for the Resurrection, like ourselves.

Ernesto Cardenal[4]

Resurrection is not just about a great splash at the end of time. The life we share has to do with 'buds of resurrection'. Faithfulness concerns becoming what we are hoping for, living out the future in the present, it includes the recognition that the process in itself is a sign, the process is 'the end in embryo', the end unfolding within, we are 'buds of resurrection'.[5]

Bishop Ting, writing from the Church in China, places resurrection truth in the social context. 'Resurrection tells us that it is through loss and poverty, suffering and death, that life is attained in nations as well as the Church. Resurrection from the dead is actually the law by which God carries on his work of the world's creation, redemption and sanctification. The principle by which the whole universe is sustained and governed.'

Jesus, we find it hard to let go false hopes and our naive notion of progress.

Jesus, hold us within the mystery of that spring that some choose to call autumn.

21

Laughter

We anticipated many things when we moved as a family to live just off the Portobello Road in Notting Hill in 1972. I did not expect to find so much laughter.[1]

She came into the vestry and asked if she could speak during the morning service in church. Later she stood up in the congregation. 'I want to say "thank you" to God. It has been a rough week both at home and at work' (and it had been). 'I have wanted to cry and I have been able to smile. I am learning to say, "Alleluia anyway, Jesus."' And the people laughed and said, 'Alleluia, praise the Lord.'

Some of the older women in the church asked, 'Where should we be on Good Friday? In church with the others or carrying the church cross to the perimeter of the nuclear base at Greenham Common?'

'What was it like?' I asked when they returned. 'We laughed,' they said, 'we laughed and we wove wool into the wire fencing to make rainbows.'

High up in the hills beyond Kingston in Jamaica I was introduced and welcomed to the small congregation as 'a friend from England'. The people spontaneously stretched under their seats for their tambourines, rose to their feet, pushed their seats back against the wall and began to sing a kind of spiritual hokey kokey. We danced, sang and laughed as I have rarely done in church. 'We are so glad that we belong to the family of God,' they sang.

On his return from a prolonged visit to South Africa and Namibia he spoke of 'the oppressed cultivating a special humour to cope with the Special Branch, a daredevil grace to laugh at things that are anything but funny'. He spoke of a multi-racial eucharist in Johannesburg cathedral as 'a piece of heaven amidst hell'. And he spoke of his meeting with Robert Sobukwe, a great and civilizing African leader, a potential leader of world stature, banned in Kimberley, yet despite imprisonment and banning he had not lost his warmth, his compassionate good humour! He spoke of Steve Biko, who detested the system yet had a strange generosity to those in authority.

On returning home after four days in the Cistercian Monastery of Mount Saint Bernard Abbey, she was asked, 'What was it like?' 'We laughed in the monastery kitchen,' she told her friends, 'and I learned that true holiness is about becoming human.'

During the signing of a Covenant between Roman Catholics, Anglicans and Methodists in a top security prison, we shared in a very correct liturgy. That is until the doors of the prison chapel opened and twelve prisoners came down the aisle holding the hands of twelve severely mentally and physically handicapped people, each carrying banners which they draped over the altar. There was then a presentation on the rainbow as a sign of promise, punctuated by little songs. After each song the congregation clapped and some privately wept and publicly laughed.

He came to our home to share his joy. He came with the news that he was going to marry. Tears flowed releasing the waters both of pain and joy. As he left our home and went down the road I saw for the first time what the Bible means when it says 'the lame leap for joy'. It was as though he set off towards the sun with an energy that was not his own!

What of joy, not happiness but joy ... the joy that comes flowing from the heart of God in response to a thankful heart ... glimpsed so often in the context of suffering?

The word 'joy' is not one that I often use. I have an intuitive suspicion of tight-lipped joy. There is a light, bright, confident, smiling, sort of Christian that makes me

tremble because the shadows seem to remain uninte-
grated, unrecognized. Once I heard a priest described
thus: 'My little priest is so bright that he borders on evil.'

Sometimes in the slot that the agenda calls 'devotions'
I like to ask: 'Where have the chuckles bubbled to the
surface for you in the last few days? Where have been
your magic moments?'

One of the shortest and most memorable letters we ever
received read thus: 'In your home there is space to
laugh!'

Conversion, for me, is as an awakening from a deep
sleep, a becoming alive, open and curious. It is an eye-
opening but an unclear seeing, an ear-opening, a hearing
not only of the cries of anguish but also of laughter, a
discovery that the world with its awesome agenda contains within it the extraordinary eucharistic testimony
'. . . heaven and earth are full of your glory'. I am dis-
covering that life is not simply to be endured but enjoyed
with a deepening sense of relish and delight both in
creation and people.

I have been taught to listen for the silence of God, to
be attentive to the suffering of God, but I have not been
taught the craft of listening for the laughter of God.

In all the world we are the free people, the celebrating, laughing ones, the ones who hug and kiss and love life, we eighty million blacks in South Africa.[2]

It is a truth well learned by all, God plays rough before breaking into laughter.

Source unidentified

Ask not always what the world needs, but what makes the heart sing.[3]

'Young man, nowhere in the New Testament is there a record that indicates that Jesus laughed.' 'But there are echoes, surely?' I said. 'Young man, there is no record.'
  Lord, have mercy!

Only slowly have I learned that the tears of penitence and joy cause the same marking on the human face. The images of 'the breaking of the waters' at a birth, as a foretaste within travail, are very precious.
  Perhaps most of us have yet to learn what it is to share in the divine contrariness of Jesus.

Only slowly have I learned to listen again to the story of old Sarah and to the testimony. 'She laughed in the face of God's promises.' But years later she said, 'God has given me good cause to laugh, and everyone who hears will laugh with me.' The child of promise born to Abraham and Sarah was called Isaac, that means 'he laughed'.[4]

If the Lord is said to veil his glory, lest it be too bright for mortal eyes, might he also veil his mirth – perhaps as something much, much too funny for men to stand?

Source unidentified

We see everything in Jesus but perhaps not his mirth.

Source unidentified

Lord, among the many words, help us to listen for your word.
Among the many paths that weave through life, help us to walk your way.
Among the many trials that at times simply have to be borne, help us to listen for the laughter of God.

Jesus: help us to hear the laughter of God even within the wounds and tears of the people, in the waiting, in the necessary patience, within the eruption of impatience.

Laughter

Jesus, give us ears for the parties.

*Jesus, lead us into the mystery that lies at the heart of
God, both the anguish and the laughter echoing from
deep among people.*

*Jesus, lay your hands on our deaf ears to hear the
music, to hear the chuckles, to hear the laughter.*

*Jesus, enable us to hear, not only the cries of the anguish,
but also the cries of joy and fulfilment.*

22

Parties

There are more parties in the Gospels and more Gospel in parties than first I realized. Be careful how you handle invitations to parties.

I was busy when he stopped me on a wind-swept corner of a street in the Golborne. I recognized the face of a young Moroccan. 'There is a party at four this afternoon under the motorway. Come, and bring a bottle and food. And pass the word around!' A spontaneous party? For whom? For Cecile. Sister Cecile was from the Sisters of the Assumption whose Convent was situated in Notting Hill near to the motorway that passes over the North Kensington landscape.

Cecile was a community nurse shortly to return to the mother house in Paris and from there she was to be directed on to a health clinic in Tunisia. She was the old nun reputed in anger and pity to have tucked up her habit, mounted her bike and gone off to the Imam in the magnificent new Mosque at Regents Park. She had made the journey in order to demand local provision for the seven thousand Moroccans, Muslims. She asked for a Mosque for the people, a place to pray.

And people came to the party carrying with them

bottles and biscuits, crisps and cakes, fruits and presents.
And they sat, their carved faces watching, Portuguese and
Moroccans, Spanish and Afro-Caribbean, social
workers, community workers, teachers, and a policeman,
people who trade in the Portobello Market and people
who wander in the back streets. In the middle of them
all Sister Cecile sat, pale and drawn, tired and stooping,
looking even older, her eyes full of love and of tears!

It was a party with all the marks of a Gospel feast.
A eucharist under a motorway!

It was a wet, windy Saturday night and there was an
invitation to leave the warm and set out towards a party.
Local Muslims were throwing a party to celebrate a
marriage. The groom was a community worker who had
worked in the area for many years. When the Muslim
community had first arrived in the area as refugees and
migrant workers, strangers in an alien country, they
looked for a place to gather, a place to pray and he
found them the St Paul's Centre. The bride was a teacher
who had travelled the world, working in Argentina,
India and Sweden. Now she worked in one of those
schools in the back streets of Birmingham, a school primarily for Asian children.

The local Muslim community wanted to say 'thank
you' as they looked back on hard days. The school hall
was a feast of cultures, dancing and singing by Indian
women in beautiful costumes, Irish folk songs, music,
including bagpipes and whistles, dance. People of very
different cultures from Pakistan, India, Ireland, Uru-

guay, Sweden, the Caribbean Islands and Britain, no longer spectators appreciating the contribution of others but participants prepared to leave their corners and to share in dance and music, women and men, young and old. The food was shared, served by men.

A most unusual encounter of humour and humanity across vast differences of culture, language and religion. A foretaste?

They had pushed off in little boats from the coast of Vietnam praying only to be washed up somewhere some day. From Hong Kong they flew to Heathrow. From Heathrow they were transported to the old convent two doors up from our home. Slowly the children came on to the streets to play. The windows opened and the washing was out . . . and also the smell of food. And a door opened and in went a letter from the neighbours to the British Council representative complaining of noise, washing and smell! And the letter was translated. And the reply was translated and carried to the neighbours. 'Come to a party – we will prepare the food, but you bring your English songs and dances!'

And some came to the party but without songs and dances. And many stayed away.

But that night people struggled with language and with chopsticks, in order to find each other. And they laughed! And something happened on that street that night to transform it.

I sensed that there was laughter both in heaven and on earth.

When the music plays during communion, that is a time to watch as people come: Doris, huffing, puffing, shuffling, smiling through her dirty glasses and lowering herself at the rail, Philip from Dominica standing silent and attentive, Enid from Jamaica gathering her grandchildren with a look that requires silence as they approach the rail, Betty approaching cautious and nervous, holding her limp and swollen arm. And others come, whilst others watch.

A foretaste? A glimpse of the banquet prepared for all people.

The Christian perception of the kingdom includes the image of a banquet prepared for all humanity to share. What does it mean to be gathered around that table with food that is common and with hands that are open to share? What does it mean to know that what we have is entrusted to us and for which we must give account? What does open-handedness mean at this table? What does bread-breaking mean as we watch exhausted refugees tread the dusty roads? Where are the signs of Gospel communism? Where are the signposts, the outbursts, the foretastes of the new world where people are liberated to share a voluntary communism?

Only slowly have I learned that on the face of Jesus there are stains, tears: stains both of grief and of joy.

Marking

Only slowly have I learned to trace the peals of laughter in the Gospels back to the parties. There are eucharistic parties, parties to say 'thank you' to God, parties thrown not in the synagogue but where things are happening within life, parties that cause scandal and offence. Where the coin that is lost is found, where the sheep that is lost is found, where the son that is lost is found, there is joy in heaven and parties on earth.

Jesus, what's this about parties?
Is it really true that you ask for 'thank you parties', eucharistic parties, thrown not in church but where it's all happening?
Parties that cause joy and offence, scandalous, seedy parties with tax gatherers, outcasts, prostitutes . . .
Perhaps someone has come clean, gone straight for longer than usual, stayed dry, said 'sorry', made peace, returned home, and there is laughter.
Lord, do you remember Levi's party . . . and the party thrown by Zacchaeus, and the tears both of penitence and of joy that stained the face?
Lord, save us from being too busy to respond to the invitations to the real parties.[1]

23

Hope: an openness to the future

Hope is trusting in a future other than the inevitable.

On Archbishop Tutu's visit to St Philip's Cathedral more stood outside than sat inside, among them a young Muslim. 'Why are you queuing to get in?' he was asked by a fervent Methodist. 'Because he is the only man in the world that I know of who speaks of hope in a way that I can trust.'

On returning from India, Bishop Lesslie Newbigin was asked what he found most difficult in Britain. 'The disappearance of hope.'[1]

The Bishop's words were echoed by a director of a huge community programme. 'Our greatest problem is not drugs, housing, race, youth alienation, but hopelessness. It is a malaise that creeps over all of us. The feeling that we can no longer change the system democratically in time. All we can offer is ambulance work and tend the wounds on the surface of society.'

It has been hard for those who have been working in some of the inner-city areas to see the result of their labours disappearing under government legislation.

Marking

The Anglican Report *Faith in the City* spoke of the abandonment of hope and asked if politicians really understood the despair which has become so widespread in so many areas.[2]

During the Gulf War, while some analysed military strategy, while some prepared to receive the injured in the Birmingham hospitals, while some protected the Mosques from possible acts of vandalism, an invitation was issued in West Bromwich to Muslims and Jews, Sikhs, Hindus and Christians to come to the Town Hall, to share silence, to read from the Holy Books, to keep vigil and afterwards to share food and develop trust within friendship.

Some accepted the invitation to attend, many recoiled from it and were too busy to attend . . . just as in the Gospel story.

But was it a bud of resurrection? – The end unfolding from within?

After only a few days working as one of the ministers in the ecumenical team in Notting Hill, someone asked me if I would make an urgent visit to a West Indian family to see the mother who, they believed, was dying and needed to make a will. I expected to find an old lady, but found in a dark, damp and depressing back room, the mother of four children, lying still and silent, while people stood watching and waiting. The will was made, prayer was offered and later in the day when I returned home, phone calls were made to doctors, social workers and housing department.

To cut a long story short, even after re-housing in a modern, centrally-heated flat, even after seeing a psychiatrist in the hospital, the woman remained strangely silent, but there were some signs of movement and awakening. On Easter Day, a few months later, the liturgy was interrupted by a large, black woman standing at the door of the church, pushing herself in on her sticks. 'The dead had come to life.' And in the months and years that followed, she learned to read and write, sang in a group at church, cared for her growing family, and assisted in the Pepper Pot, a Day Centre under the motorway helping with cooking and craft-work for lonely, elderly Afro-Caribbean people.

It is not easy within the social travail of this country to see 'the birth pangs of a new age'. There are, however, signs! They are glimpses through those in whom we recognize something of the divine contrariness of Jesus, those who shivered and suffered in peace camps such as the Rainbow Village at Molesworth, those who uncover the truth that many would prefer to keep hidden, those who dare to believe that oppressive systems can and will be broken, those who dare to believe in the uprising of the downtrodden, those who dare to be free within so much that polarizes and paralyses within society. I have discovered within the social travail a new faith in resurrection. It is the nature of the living God to bring life out of death, to lift up the downtrodden.

Dare we believe that the future can be any different from what we fear ? Could the future unfold and hold meaning? Could it provide a threshold where we will one day testify 'God has brought us to this place?'

The testimony to dying and rising can slip off our tongues naively, easily. That is until you look into the faces of those whose bodies bear the process of transition. It is right, I believe, to keep asking, 'What new thing is God wanting to bring into being among us that can only be discovered when we are prepared to loosen our grip on the past?'

Learning to let go so that God can take us to places beyond our own planning belongs to the nature of our journey from, in and towards God.

Social despair eats into the soul of many Western countries. For some of us the awakening of idealism and social hope was integral to our early Christian experience. We offered to God our plans for society, our resources, our commitment, but what we hoped for, prayed and struggled for in society has largely not happened. Some of us have grown tired, disillusioned and have lost social hope. Disappointment is an important element in resurrection hope.

To speak of the renewal of vision without acknowledging the reality of that disappointment and disillusion which leads to social disengagement will be to hide from reality. This is a matter of soul both for people and community. Christian hope requires that we painfully let go false hopes and naive notions of progress. The biblical testimony is that it is the very nature of God to bring life amongst the ruins of shattered dreams and failures.

There is a testimony to God of a timorous, tentative nature made through people whose circumstances have brought them to an unfamiliar place in human experience, a territory that requires crossing that necessitates trusting the unknown. This is the place of crossing, a territory that you may not control, it is the place both of longing and fear, but also the place of disclosure.

It is a place where the fragments of broken images are gathered and integrated into a new mosaic.

For years I have lived with 'social hope' and in the middle years discovered that much we had hoped and prayed for, struggled and suffered for, has not happened as we planned. Early assumptions about social change, about people, about myself, about the Church and God have been exposed as naive. I have learnt that disappointment can lead to disengagement. Only slowly have I glimpsed the difference between social hope and resurrection hope ... the hope beyond hope that is rooted in the very nature of God who makes all things new.

Today there is no room for mystery in Sweden. Our hope lies within the arrival of the Orthodox Church among the refugees. They speak to us both of mystery and of resurrection.[3]

We take the road empty handed, without a map to guide us . . . cast off hope if you have it. The burden of hope is too heavy. The way itself knows where it is going. The way itself will lift us forward. The way itself is all.

Source unidentified

Hope liberates from expectation. It is centred in the endlessly creative power of God to generate new things, to draw life out of death. To live in hope rather than expectation is to live wholly in the present moment. It is to look to the future as unexpected gift.[4]

I believe in a world that does not exist but by believing in it, I create it.

Source unidentified

Jesus, lead us through disappointment and disillusionment to hope. Deepen our trust in the God who brings life among the ruins.

Hope: *an openness to the future*

Jesus, thank you for those women and men,
people of passion and compassion,
people belonging to the villages, towns and cities of the
  world,
people who, within the reality of so much suffering,
  despair and destruction,
dare to believe that tomorrow can be different,
and who carry in their bodies the marks of that hope.
For them we both give thanks and pray.

24

Transformation

I believe that the purity, perfection trip is highly danger-ous for it denies the significance and potency of shadow. Shadow can be the context of the transformation of evil into good.

I arrived home one night to discover my wife watching the second showing of the programme from the orphan-age in Romania with Anneka Rice. It showed not only the transformation of appalling old buildings, the trans-formation of pathetically neglected children, but also ordinary people from the West Midlands who had gone out to help: plumbers, electricians, builders and carpen-ters. They also were transformed.

She was young, black, beautiful and on a visit to Birm-ingham. She was with her friends in a pub and whilst they talked, the door of the pub swung open. 'Shift, you black bastard!' She stood slowly, arched herself like a black cat ready to let loose an almost historic spitting fury. After a long silence that I still find it hard to believe could happen, her face broke into a smile. Later in a confirmation class she told us, 'For me to behave like an animal would only confirm what they already thought of us, and from somewhere deep down I found a smile of pity.' What a victory!

What a confirmation!

During the period in hospital, I caught a glimpse of something I find it hard to express. It happens within those jagged and rough territories of human experience that include all the possibilities of the negative and the destructive but also hold the potential for deepening, growing and responding.

I began to wonder whether prayer releases among us and within us a 'yes' to life, an openness to the reality of our human experience with all its swirling powers both for destruction and creation, a willingness to turn into those territories that we would under normal circumstances wish to withdraw from, a capacity to open ourselves and enter an exploration.

Perhaps this has something to do with the nature of trust. We enter the waters not knowing in quite what form we will be washed up on the other side nor where, or if we arrive at all. For a moment I became aware of what transformation could be about.

Years ago I read a phrase in a book that affected me deeply, but when I came to look for it later I couldn't find it. It was something like this: 'the transformation of evil into good through forgiveness and love'. Was it Mahatma Gandhi or Martin Luther King making their own testimony to structural transformation through non-violent action?

I discovered later that the words came from Thomas Merton. 'Evil is reversible and can be changed into good by forgiveness and love.' Here lies, I believe, the mystery that brings us to a proper trembling. This is the mystery that we glimpse on the cross and discloses the heart of God.

The vocation we live is not just discerning, but integrating and not just integrating, but transforming. Deeply-rooted evil within the created order has not only to be recognized but also to be cast out. Most of us are slow to recognize that the evil, sin, and violence which we see in the world and in other people is in reality deeply-rooted within our own hearts.

Margaret Spufford writes as one living not only with the physical pain of her own incurable disease but also as one who has lived with the mental pain of her daughter's incurable disease. 'One of the most helpful things that was ever said to me was "The definition of 'Almighty' means that there is no evil out of which good cannot be brought." This I have found, extremely painfully, to be true.'[1]

'Here we offer and present to you, O Lord, ourselves, our souls and bodies to be a reasonable, holy and living sacrifice . . .'[2]

Transformation

Such a familiar prayer, yet transformed when uttered by a person whose pilgrimage includes physical pain.

The task, say the liberation theologians, is not simply to recognize and to understand injustice, but to bring it to an end. Theology is not in the business of explanation, but transformation.

The philosophers have only interpreted the world in various ways; the point, however, is to change it.

Karl Marx[3]

The mystery we enter is evil transformed, suffering converted into good for the sake of others.

Terry Waite[4]

The cross is the new model of salvation, not a rescue like the exodus from an evil situation, but plumbing the depths of separation, failure, denial and forsakenness. We are not offered salvation from an evil situation, but salvation in and through an evil situation, first confronting it, then bearing it and transforming it. It is as if evil is the raw material out of which new life is forged. The news of the Gospel is not moral perfection nor sinlessness, it is forgiveness. Jesus is less interested in the causes of evil than in its transformation.

Michael Wilson[5]

> Stand still in the pain,
> rooted in that in you which is light.
> Let the sword go through you.
> Maybe it is not
> a sword at all.
> Maybe it is a tuning fork.
> You become a note.
> You become the music
> you always longed
> to hear.
> You didn't know that you were
> a song.
>
> Ylva Eggehorn[6]

Jesus, you recognize evil both in our structures and in our hearts; you expose it; you confront it but more, you offer to transform it. Lead us into this mystery and hold us in our trembling.

Jesus, show us your cross, lead us into those paths that will lead to the transforming of nations, communities and ourselves, give us courage in our weakness.

Transformation

Jesus, we stumble in the dark, You are the light of the world, transform us.
Spirit of God we forget that we are your home.
Spirit of God, dwell in us.

Jesus, in your body we catch a glimpse of the terrible travail at the heart of all life.
Evil is reversible, evil can be changed into good, principalities and powers can be transformed through forgiveness and love.
Help us to see that deeply rooted evil in the created order has not only to be named but transformed.
Draw us into the mystery of that awesome festival.

References

WAITING

1 Waiting

1. W.H. Vanstone, *The Stature of Waiting*, Darton, Longman and Todd 1982, p.83.
2. In conversation with Michael Wilson. Michael was an Anglican priest who worked as a medical doctor in Ghana. He was Chaplain of the Guild of Health before taking up the post of Lecturer at St Martin the Fields in London. He pioneered pastoral studies in the Department of Theology at the Birmingham University. He has been for many, including myself, both friend and guide over many years. He died early in the morning of Saturday 20 March 1999.
3. A guestmaster in a monastery.
4. A commercial slogan.
5. See W.H. Vanstone, *The Stature of Waiting*, ch.6, 'The God Who Waits'.
6. Ibid., pp.111–12.
7. Ibid., p.70.
8. Daniel Day Williams, *The Spirit and the Forms of Love*, James Nisbett 1968, p.14.
9. In conversation with Michael Wilson.
10. From a retreat address on providence given by Jean Vanier.
11. See Esther de Waal, *Living with Contradiction*, Collins Fount 1989; reissued Canterbury Press 1997, pp.119f. See also her *A*

References

Life-Giving Way, A Commentary on the Rule of St Benedict,
Geoffrey Chapman 1995, p.11.

12. R.S.Thomas, 'Kneeling', *Collected Poems 1945–1990*, J.M.
Dent 1993, p.199.
13. Henri J.M. Nouwen, *Seeds of Hope*, Darton Longman and Todd
1989, p.105.

2 Silence

1. The caption on a poster of a beautiful country scene.
2. From a letter.
3. In conversation with Michael Wilson.
4. Elizabeth Jennings, 'Distractions', *Tributes*, Carcanet 1989,
p.112.
5. Developed from Wendy Robinson, *Exploring Silence*, Fairacres
Publications 1974, p.9
6. Lao Tsu, *Tao Te Ching*, sixth century. This quotation came to
me via Michael Wilson.
7. In conversation with Michael Wilson.
8. Nicholas Lash, *A Matter of Hope: A Theologian's Reflections
on the Thought of Karl Marx*, Darton Longman and Todd 1981,
p.193.
9. Wisdom 18.14.

3 A silence beyond anger

1. A community worker in an urban priority project in Handsworth. He was describing a sense of despair leading to power-
lessness after yet another round of cuts in funding.

4 The everyday place

1. From an address given by Archbishop Desmond Tutu during
the week when he led *The City-wide Christian Celebration* in
Birmingham in April 1989.
2. R.S.Thomas, 'Pilgrimages,' *Collected Poems 1945–1990*, J.M.
Dent 1993, p.364.
3. A celtic prayer taken from *Flowing Streams. An Anthology of*

References

Anthologies compiled by Donald Hilton, National Christian Education Council 1993, p.111.

4. A passage read at the funeral of Helen Noakes in 1992.
5. See Genesis 28.16, REB.
6. From a conversation during a period when Emmanuel Jacob was in Britain studying for his Doctorate in Liberation Studies at Bristol University. Emmanuel is a Methodist Minister from South Africa.
7. For a development of this theme see Esther de Waal, *Seeking God*, Collins Fount 1984, pp.99–111.

5 Waiting among people

1. R.E.C. Browne, unpublished papers. R.E.C. Browne was one-time Study Secretary for the Student Christian Movement, author of *The Ministry of the Word* (SCM Press 1958) and parish priest in the diocese of Manchester.
2. From a conversation with Father Michael Hollings. Michael was a Roman Catholic parish priest in Bayswater.
3. Leonard Cohen, 'Stranger Music,' *Selected Poems and Songs*, Jonathan Cape 1993.
4. See John 9.25, REB.
5. See Luke 16.20.
6. R. E. C. Browne, unpublished papers.

6 Waiting for healing

1. In conversation with Michael Wilson and quoting the psycho-analyst Groddeck.
2. David Stacey, writing from his home in Cambridge.
3. In conversation with Michael Wilson.
4. In conversation with Michael Wilson and quoting Dr Bernie Segal.
5. See John 5.6, REB.
6. From a local liturgy prepared by David Blanchflower.

References

7 Anger

1. Archbishop Desmond Tutu during his visit to share in *The City-wide Christian Celebration* in Birmingham in April 1989.
2. See Exodus 2.11f. and Exodus 3.1f.
3. A line from a Negro Spiritual, 'Home in that Rock' in James Baldwin, *The Fire Next Time*, Penguin 1964, p. 89.
4. Developed from Pierre Teilhard de Chardin, *Hymn of the Universe*, Collins Fontana 1965, p.21.
5. Maya Angelou in conversation on BBC Radio 4
6. In a letter from a friend.

8 Travail

1. In conversation with Michael Wilson.
2. In 1987 Alan Kirton was the General Secretary of the Caribbean Council of Churches. He is a Methodist minister.
3. From a conversation with a friend from Zimbabwe following a vigil of prayer in Birmingham Cathedral during the Gulf War.
4. Metusalem was a young exile studying at the Selly Oak Colleges and waiting to return to Namibia after many years in refugee camps.
5. A Chinese curse.
6. Jeremiah 2.8, REB.
7. See Matthew 25.31–46.
8. A personal reflection in response to Lesslie Newbigin's book *The Other Side Of 1984*, Risk Series, WCC, Geneva 1984.
9. John V. Taylor, *The Christlike God*, SCM Press 1992, p.224.
10. Brendan Kennelly, 'Willow', *A Time for Voices: Selected Poems 1960–1990*, Bloodaxe Books 1990.
11. A prayer from the World Council of Churches.

9 Deaths in life

1. In conversation with Michael Wilson.
2. Inderjit Bhogal is now a Methodist minister living and working in Sheffield.
3. Michael Smith, printed in *Helen House News*, Spring 95, No. 27, Vol. 2217.

References

4. From a conversation between a father and daughter.
5. From a conversation with an old man waiting to die.
6. Taken from a letter from a friend.
7. *Mud and Stars*, The Report of a Working Party on the Impact of Hospice Experience on the Church's Ministry of Healing, Sobell Publications 1991, p.37.
8. Ibid., p.38.
9. Ibid., p.41.
10. Ibid., p.42.
11. From a letter received from Celsus, a Cistercian monk, during a period when I was very tired. Celsus was at the time Guest Master at the Monastery of Mount St Bernard Abbey, near Coalville in Leicestershire.
12. The quotation is from Wendy Robinson, *Exploring Silence*, Fairacres Publications 1974, p. 4.
13. A prayer based on Pierre Teilhard de Chardin, Pensées 90, *Hymn of the Universe*, Collins 1965, p.94.

TRUSTING

10 Trusting

1. André Brink, *The Chain of Voices*, Faber 1982, p.497.
2. A young person on returning from a visit to the Caribbean.
3. In conversation with Michael Wilson.
4. Mary Worrall.
5. A poem that seems to have been part of the personal correspondence of Pierre Teilhard de Chardin. The translator is unknown.
6. A prayer by R.G. Jones from *The Methodist Prayer Handbook*, Methodist Publishing House 1987.

11 Openness

1. Max Warren in the General Introduction to Kenneth Cragg, *Sandals at the Mosque. Christian Presence amid Islam*, SCM Press 1959, p.9.

2. The prayer of a Muslim woman after concluding a meeting on migration and asylum issues in Handsworth.

12 *Holding*

1. Abel Hendricks is a Methodist minister in South Africa.
2. From a conversation.
3. Advice given to the parents of lively teenagers.
4. David Brown, *A New Threshold*, BCC 1976, p.21.
5. An old prayer, *teneo et teneor.*

13 *Friendship*

1. This is a translation of a slogan daubed on to walls of an underground station in Stockhom in an area where people from over fifty different nationalities live. In that city we listened to stories of what can happen when people dare to open their homes, share their food and sit in each other's gardens.
2. Janet Morley, *Bread of Tomorrow*, Christian Aid/SPCK 1992, p.38.

14 *Turning*

1. R.S.Thomas, 'Mass for Hard Times', from *Mass for Hard Times*, Bloodaxe Books 1992, p.12.
2. Laurens van der Post, *The Lost World of the Kalahari*, Penguin 1962, p.171.
3. Found on the wall of an Ashram.
4. From a BBC radio commentary on the occasion when the Bishop of Coventry accompanied the Queen to Dresden.
5. See Genesis 18.11.
6. See Acts 11.
7. A prayer used during the concluding act of worship at the 1991 Malvern Conference. The first such conference was held in 1941, brought into being by the great William Temple when still Archbishop of York.
8. A prayer written and used by Ian Fraser during a retreat for Methodist ministers.
9. Russell Maltby, 'A Greeting' in *The Agenda* (organ of the Wesley

Deaconess Order of the Methodist Church), December 1940, p.11.

15 *The place of testing*

1. For further reading on Thomas Merton see Henri Nouwen, *Thomas Merton – contemplative critic*, Harper and Row 1981.
2. William Axling, *Kagawa*, SCM Press 1932, p.151. 'This mystic' is Toyohiki Kagawa, a man who lived for fifteen years in Shinkawi in a six by six labourer's hut. He strove to stem the downward drift of the lives around him. Axling is quoting here from Kagawa's own *Meditations*. I re-read the book in one day whilst waiting for treatment in the day hospital.

MARKING

16 *The body*

1. See John 1.14.
2. See Genesis 33.10.
3. Henri Nouwen, *Seeds of Hope*, Darton, Longman and Todd 1989, p.118.
4. Frances Croake Frank, Extract 99 in *Celebrating Women*, Hannah Ward, Jennifer Wild and Janet Morley (eds), SPCK 1995.
5. John 21.12, REB.
6. Dietrich Bonhoeffer, 'Prayers for Fellow Prisoners', *Letters and Papers from Prison*, The Enlarged Edition, SCM Press 1971, p.139.

17 *The growing place*

1. Maya Angelou in conversation on BBC Radio 4.
2. Lao Tsu, *Tao Te Ching*, 76. This version was given to me by a friend; it is based on a new translation by Gia-Fu Feng and Jane English, Wildwood House 1973.

References

3. Karin Boye, 'Yes, of course it hurts', *Complete Poems*, translated by David McDuff, Bloodaxe Books 1994, p.119.

18 Unfolding

1. See John 10.1–18.
2. See I Kings 17. 4.
3. In conversation with Michael Wilson and quoting William Sloan Coffin.

19 Witholding

1. 'God moves in a mysterious way', hymn 65 in *Hymns and Psalms*.
2. Michael Wilson, 'The answer's no', an unpublished poem.
3. See Matthew 5.1–16.
4. See Luke 1.46–55.
5. Overheard in a period of shared quiet during the Gulf War.
6. Jim Cotter, 'A new unfolding of Psalm 77' in *By Stony Paths*, Cairns Publications 1991, p.55.

20 Life

1. Nicene Creed.
2. Margaret Torrie, *Selected Poems*, published privately, p.5. Margaret Torrie is the founder of Cruse Bereavement Care.
3. See Luke 24.21.
4. Ernesto Cardenal, 'Behind the monastery,' *Marilyn Monroe and other Poems*, Search Press 1975, p.60.
5. From a conversation with Michael Wilson.

21 Laughter

1. Notting Hill at that time had an estimated population of 80,000 people living in one and a quarter square miles. It had a reputation in the media for being a multi-problem area.
2. Robert Sobukwe, who was elected President when the Pan Africanist Congress came into being on 6 April 1959. He was a fellow prisoner with Nelson Mandela.

References

3. A slogan on the wall in the room of a severely handicapped young man.
4. See Genesis 21.6a.

22 Parties

1. See Luke 19.1–10.

23 Hope: an openness to the future

1. Lesslie Newbigin, *The Other Side of 1984*, Risk Books, WCC, Geneva 1984, p.1.
2. *Faith in the City* (A Call for Action by Church and Nation), Church House Publishing 1985.
3. A Finnish social worker based in Stockholm.
4. Found in a flat belonging to a small community of Roman Catholic nuns living in Heathtown, Wolverhampton.

24 Transformation

1. The quotation is from Margaret Spufford, *Celebration*, Collins Fount 1989, p.80.
2. From *The Book of Offices*, Methodist Publishing House 1936, p.85.
3. Karl Marx, *Thesis on Feuerbach no. 11*, published in 1888. This aphorism appears on his grave in Highgate cemetery.
4. Terry Waite during a radio interview.
5. Michael Wilson, from an unpublished essay entitled 'God of Love and Evil'.
6 .A rough translation by Kerstin Eadie from the Swedish of the poem by Ylva Eggehorn, 'Stå stilla i smärtan', *Att Bejaka Sin Längtan*, Verbum Förlag.

Acknowledgments

I am grateful to the following for permission to include copyright material:

To Bloodaxe Books for R.S. Thomas's poem 'Mass for Hard Times' from *Mass for Hard Times*, 1992; for Karin Boye's 'Yes, of course it hurts' from *Complete Poems*, 1994; and for Brendan Kennelly's 'Willow' from *A Time for Voices: Selected Poems 1960–1990*, 1990.

To Cherry Bowen for Margaret Torrie's poem 'Via Dolorosa', *Selected Poems*.

To Jonathan Cape for Leonard Cohen, 'Stranger Music' from *Selected Poems and Songs*, 1993.

To Carcanet for Elizabeth Jennings, 'Distractions' from *Tributes*, 1989, p.112.

To Jim Cotter for 'A prayer in response to a new unfolding of Psalm 77' in *By Stony Paths*, Cairns Publications 1991, p.55.

To the Centre Teilhard de Chardin in Paris for the poem by Teilhard de Chardin.

To Ylva Eggehorn for her poem 'Stå stilla i smärtan' (Stand still in the pain) in a rough translation by Kerstin Eadie.

Acknowledgments

To the Orion Publishing Group for R. S. Thomas's poems 'Kneeling' and 'Pilgrimages' from *Collected Poems 1945–1990*, J.M. Dent 1993.

To SCM Press for extracts from John V. Taylor, The *Christlike God*, 1992; William Axling, *Kagawa*, 1932; and Dietrich Bonhoeffer, *Letters and Papers from Prison*, 1971.

To Search Press Ltd for Ernesto Cardenal, 'Behind the monastery' from *Marilyn Monroe and other Poems*, 1975.

To SPCK for Frances Croake Frank, 'Did the women say ...' from *Celebrating Women*, Hannah Ward, Jennifer Wild and Janet Morley (eds), 1995; and for the prayer from Janet Morley's *Bread of Tomorrow*, 1992.

To Inderjit Bhogal, David Blanchflower, Ian Fraser, Emmanuel Jacob, Richard Jones, Michael Wilson and Mary Worrall for permission to use prayers, poems and parts of conversations.

To Husmo-foto in Bildearvik in Norway for permission to use the photograph on the front cover of this book.

Every effort has been made to trace the copyright holders of the quoted extracts, but a few remain for which the source is not known. The publisher would be glad to hear from the copyright holders of such extracts, so that appropriate acknowledgment can be made in any future edition of this book.